Maimonides' Grand Epistle to the Scholars of Lunel: Ideology and Rhetoric

Maimonides' Grand Epistle to the Scholars of Lunel: Ideology and Rhetoric

CHARLES H. SHEER

BOSTON
2019

Library of Congress Cataloging-in-Publication Data
Names: Sheer, Charles H., author.
Title: Maimonides' grand epistle to the scholars of Lunel : ideology and
   rhetoric / Charles H. Sheer.
Description: Boston, MA : Academic Studies Press, 2019. | Includes
   bibliographical references.
Identifiers: LCCN 2018057556 (print) | LCCN 2018059382 (ebook) | ISBN
   9781618119629 (ebook) | ISBN 9781618119605 (hardcover) | ISBN
   9781618119612 (pbk.)
Subjects: LCSH: Maimonides, Moses, 1135-1204. Correspondence. |
   Responsa–1040-1600. | Hebrew language–Prosodic analysis. |
   Prosodic   analysis (Linguistics) | Jewish scholars–France–Lunel–
   Correspondence.
Classification: LCC BM755.M6 (ebook) | LCC BM755.M6 A4 2019 (print) | DDC
   296.1/81–dc23
LC record available at https://lccn.loc.gov/2018057556

On the cover: R. Jonathan's second letter, Bodleian Library, Genizah Fragments.
   Reproduced by permission.

©Academic Studies Press, 2019
ISBN 978-1-618119-60-5 (hardback)
ISBN 978-1-618119-61-2 (paperback)
ISBN 978-1-618119-62-9 (electronic)

Book design by Lapiz Digital Services

Published by Academic Studies Press
28 Montfern Avenue
Brighton, MA 02135, USA
press@academicstudiespress.com
www.academicstudiespress.com

To
Judy Adler Sheer
My *ḥavruta* (partner) in life and learning

Contents

Preface	viii
Introduction	xi
Maimonides and the Lunel Scholars	xi
The Correspondence between Maimonides and French Scholars	xv
1) Maimonides' Grand *Iggeret* to R. Jonathan of Lunel	1
2) The First Half of the *Iggeret* in Rhymed Prose	7
3) Maimonides' Unanticipated and Problematic Style Reversal	16
4) Maimonides' Letter to Judge Anatoli	21
5) The Letters from R. Jonathan of Lunel	24
6) The Second Half of the *Iggeret* in Unadorned Prose	38
7) Maimonides and the Lunel Scholars—Reconsidered	51
Appendix	58
Endnotes	69

Preface

A Judaica bookseller, knowing my interest in all things Maimonidean, recommended I purchase a slim volume that contained a photocopy of a translation of 150 responsa by Maimonides. This translation was the principal entry into the responsa of the Great Master until around fifty years ago, when Prof. Joshua Blau presented his four-volume collection of Maimonides' responsa. *P'er HaDor* was printed in Amsterdam in 1765. Its title page noted that this manuscript had been a "precious hidden treasure" for years since it was written in Arabic and very few people had been able to read it.[1]

My bookseller was correct. I was fascinated by the anthology. Unfortunately, only a few of the responsa were dated, and few recorded the name of the correspondent. I missed not being able to place the letters in historic context or locale. But the translator, R. Mordechai Tammah, often cited the location where Maimonides treated the topic of each responsum in the *Mishneh Torah,* his great *Hibbur*—Compilation or Law Code, as he called it in its Introduction. Due to my acquisition of *P'er HaDor*, I gained new insight into Maimonides' legal mind and how he moved from Talmudic sources to codified law and actual practice. The book enhanced my appreciation for the awesome scholarship of Maimonides and his role as a teacher and rabbinic decisor.

Most of the responsa were brief letters in which Maimonides rendered his decision in terse language. Few were extended discourses. But suddenly, as I made my way through this anthology, I encountered a responsum by the Grand Rabbi that differed from all others I had studied. Its opening line was not a Talmudic passage or case presentation. Maimonides began his rejoinder with a verse from Isaiah. Many of the subsequent lines also sounded like biblical passages, but when I looked at them more closely, I discovered that many diverged slightly from the original as found in the *Tanakh* (Hebrew Scriptures). Maimonides had modified many biblical lines; furthermore, many words in his responsum were not in accord with Hebrew grammar.

To my great surprise, I discovered that within the context of a rabbinic correspondence, Maimonides had fashioned what is called a rhymed prose epistle. This elegant letter served as a header to a series of responsa he wrote to a group of Provencal Jews.

My first goal was to understand this *Iggeret*. Interpreting its complex language was a challenge. Beyond that, I wished to ascertain what stimulated this unusual composition. What was the relationship between Maimonides and these Lunel scholars that brought him to write to them in this fashion? Additionally, I was not aware that the author of the *Mishneh Torah* and *Guide of the Perplexed* had engaged in this genre of poetic composition.

This book entails a close examination of this composition. I will demonstrate that an essential aspect of Maimonides' communication to this community is conveyed by the style of the epistle. As I worked through the letter and unpacked its complex images, sources, and ideas, I gained a new appreciation for Maimonides' genius.

I wish to acknowledge many who assisted me in my study of this work. First, I thank Raymond P. Scheindlin (Prof. Emeritus of Medieval Hebrew Literature, Jewish Theological Seminary) who read my initial draft and directed me to various works regarding medieval Jewish poetry and literature. His guidance at the start of my research was invaluable. Josef Stern (William H. Colvin Prof. of Philosophy Emeritus, University of Chicago) reviewed the first version of the manuscript, offering detailed comments about the draft and the overall direction of my research. Both scholars were helpful and generous with their time. I thank them for their insights, suggestions, and encouragement.

When my book was nearing completion, I undertook another search to ascertain if new scholarship had been published subsequent to the conclusion of my research. To my great delight, that investigation led me to Jonathan Decter (Edmond J. Safra Prof. of Sephardic Studies, Brandeis University), who generously shared with me relevant chapters of a forthcoming book, *Dominion Built of Praise: Panegyric and Legitimacy among Jews in the Medieval Mediterranean*, being published by University of Pennsylvania Press. His scholarship greatly enhanced my work, and I thank him for his collegial support by granting me permission to cite from his book.[2]

I thank the Senior Editor at Academic Studies Press, Alessandra Anzani, who carefully oversaw the preparation of my book. I greatly appreciated the fine editorial skills of Eileen Wolfberg, Editorial Coordinator, who worked diligently to ensure that the final product was worthy of the careful reading that Maimonides valued (see his *Commentary to the Mishnah*, Hagigah 3:2, as quoted on page xiii of this book.) My research was ably assisted by the librarians of the Mendel Gottesman Library at Yeshiva University. I also wish to acknowledge the encouragement and active involvement of David Adler, of Passaic, New Jersey. He enthusiastically urged me to convert my research on this topic into written form and connected me with Mitch Morrison, who facilitated the publication of this book.

I am indebted to my wife, Judy Adler Sheer, who reviewed much of the book over its many years of gestation and was a keen critic of its form and content. This book is dedicated to her as an expression of my affection and appreciation for the many aspects of my life that have been enriched by her.

Introduction

Maimonides and the Lunel Scholars

Maimonides completed his *Mishneh Torah* (henceforth, MT) between the end of 1177 and the beginning of 1178.[3] In subsequent decades, it was disseminated to centers of Jewish learning in communities throughout the medieval Jewish world. When it reached Southern France—probably not before 1193[4]—a circle of scholars in Lunel eagerly studied Maimonides' *Hibbur*. Although they readily noted the remarkable scholarship of the author and his astounding mastery of the full corpus of rabbinic literature—I shall have many occasions below to quote their laudatory statements about Maimonides—these scholars found various places in the MT where they disagreed with Maimonides' decision. When it came to the interpretation of Talmudic texts and normative aspects of Jewish law, the Lunel rabbis stood on the backs of generations of Provencal scholars who had their own traditions and scholarly positions.[5] They compiled a set of twenty-four questions that were sent to him under the name of the leader of the circle, R. Jonathan ben David HaKohen.[6]

The Lunel questions differed from the inquiries Maimonides received from individuals, communities, other scholars, and rabbinic courts, most of which were actual cases submitted for Maimonides' judgment, often as an ultimate court of appeal.[7] Although some of the twenty-four questions focused on ritual observance and personal practice—such as liturgy, Sabbath regulations, dietary laws, vows, and sexual relations—the stimulus for this set of questions was Maimonides' MT—his Code of Jewish Law. These questions were within the arena of Talmudic scholarship and textual analysis, not practical jurisprudence.

The Twenty-Four were a favored set that Maimonides cherished—I will present his remarks to this effect below—and they were already well known in the generation of Maimonides' son, R. Abraham, who recorded his father's joy at their receipt.⁸ Most of the classical commentators to the *Mishneh Torah* discussed these responsa⁹; historians and critical scholars analyzed the history and development of this exchange, as will be illustrated throughout this study. These twenty-four questions are the most well-known of Maimonides' responsa.¹⁰

In the context of studying Maimonides' responsa, I came upon his correspondence with the Lunel scholars. With much excitement, I began to study his rejoinder to this set, expecting that the Grand Master would follow the usual method of scholarly argumentation. I assumed he would briefly review the Lunel critique of his *Mishneh Torah* and then rebut their positions based upon his interpretation of Talmudic passages and Geonic opinions. I assumed that Maimonides' rejoinder would entail an in-depth analysis of Talmudic material. I was unprepared for what I found.

Maimonides, of course, did author responses to their twenty-four questions. However, prior to his responsa, he presented the Lunel scholars with a magnificent fifty-nine-line epistle (Blau edition) written in grand poetic style. The initial half was an elegantly crafted rhymed prose composition, written in complex Hebrew, often incorporating—and frequently modifying—biblical passages or Midrashic texts.

Many of the lines are exceedingly difficult to interpret. Maimonides' images were complex, requiring knowledge of biblical and rabbinic texts. Also, when referring to his Lunel interlocutors, he used extremely exaggerated language, artfully fashioning effusive and laudatory remarks about these men. Then, suddenly after thirty lines of rhymed prose, Maimonides continued his letter in non-rhymed prose, following the more customary rhetoric for such compositions.

This *Iggeret* apparently served as an epistolary header for his scholarly response. Within this composition, he did not respond to the questions asked by the Lunel scholars nor did he treat the subjects of their enquiry.

This literary composition stimulated a number of questions for me. I knew that the rhymed prose segment was composed in a poetic style developed in the late Middle Ages, which became normative in various countries and cultures. I will discuss this genre later in this study. However, I was not aware of Maimonides' engagement in this kind of composition, especially in the context of a scholarly exchange dealing with Talmudic law. In the hundreds of responsa by Maimonides that I had studied, as well as in his voluminous compositions in Jewish law and philosophy, I was not aware of another instance when he incorporated a substantial rhymed prose composition within his work.

Many authors during the medieval period and beyond opened their works with a poetic composition.[11] Maimonides himself composed a brief proem at the start of his *Commentary to the Mishnah*. However, the size of this epistle, its stylistic complexity, and its independence from the responsa set it apart from his proem in his *Commentary to the Mishnah* and similar poetic introductions by rabbinic authors.

Was this epistle a unique composition by the Great Sage? If so, what stimulated it? I sought to ascertain if there were other Maimonidean writings in which the master of Talmudic Law and philosophy displayed an artistic bent.

There was another aspect of this epistle that needed to be considered, which relates to its rhetorical nature. Throughout his works, Maimonides placed much importance on his compositional style, choice of language, and clarity of expression.[12] In his *Commentary to the Mishnah*, Hagigah 3:2, he wrote:

> And if you wish to have all-encompassing understanding [of the laws] of Impurity and Purity, examine carefully our words on that Order [i.e., section of the Mishnah] from beginning to end. And do not read them hastily and superficially; rather, read them thoroughly and with careful reflection.

How did this rhymed prose epistle fit within Maimonides' compositional guidelines? His exaggerated depictions of his Lunel correspondents and the words he used to laud their writings would not withstand the thorough, careful, and reflective reading Maimonides treasured. As I shall discuss below, such panegyric compositions, as they are called, were crafted intentionally with exaggerated and effusive language. Many lines in his *Iggeret* were written in a style that contradicted his declared values. When he enjoined his readers to "examine carefully our words" and "read them thoroughly and with careful reflection," did he intend to invite his readers to subject this rhymed prose epistle to the same scrupulous analysis?

Maimonides' epistle was translated by Leon D. Stitskin and Isadore Twersky. Stitskin included it in his "Letters of Maimonides" with a brief introduction.[13] Twersky discussed Maimonides' letter to R. Jonathan in his "Introduction to the Code of Maimonides" and offered a translation.[14] These translations differ from mine in size and objective. Stitskin sought to convey the essential themes of the letter. A simple comparison between his text and either Twersky's or mine will illustrate that he neglected to translate many sentences or words in the original. His version frequently does not convey the style or language of Maimonides' letter, and hardly intimates its biblical or Midrashic sources.

Twersky translated the prose part of the *Iggeret* as we have it in the original and identified biblical passages that were cited in full. My translation was enhanced by his. However, an essential objective of my study will be to discover the sources with which Maimonides built his letter. In both parts of his epistle, Maimonides developed formulations that were adaptations from scriptural or rabbinic texts. In many cases, I have deliberately translated his text to reveal the textual underpinnings upon which Maimonides artfully fashioned his composition.

More important, the translations presented by Stitskin and Twersky are approximately one-half the size of mine. Both started their translation at the midpoint of the epistle, where Maimonides shifted from rhymed to standard prose. They ignored entirely the first half, possibly because they viewed it as a mere artistic embellishment.[15]

I will argue that Maimonides' stylistic shift was not merely an artistic enhancement to vary the rhetoric of his letter. I will demonstrate that Maimonides' statements in this epistle—and his other communications with the Lunel scholars—indicated that he deliberately authored a composite epistle to convey a vital message to his Lunel correspondents.

In his *Iggeret*, Maimonides shared with his correspondents some of his deeply held convictions. He included personal information about his life and his aspirations for his legacy, along with the role these men might play in it. The ideas that Maimonides marshaled in his epistle in distinctive and memorable fashion suggest that it warrants a special place within his writings. It should be appreciated as a valuable element in our understanding of the intellectual life and thought of Maimonides. It reveals much about the heart and mind of this towering figure and provides an intellectual and historical portrait of him during the last decade of his life.

The character of any correspondence is shaped, in part, by the relationship between the participants in the exchange. Before I present the translation of Maimonides' epistle, I shall review what is known about the relationship between Maimonides and the Lunel scholars.

The Correspondence between Maimonides and French Scholars

The Lunel correspondence was not the first inquiry by a French community to Maimonides. In a prior communication, scholars from the city of Montpellier solicited Maimonides' opinion regarding the status of astrology in Judaism.[16] They were perplexed by contradictory sources regarding the acceptability of astrology in Jewish thought. They cited various Talmudic[17] and Midrashic passages implying that the ancient rabbis believed that astrological factors (*mazal*) could determine the destinies of individuals and nations. On the other hand, other classical sources seemed to reject this idea. The French scholars noted that Geonim had treated this question as well. However, since his correspondents had only modest training in "*hokhmah*" (worldly knowledge or philosophy), they turned to Maimonides "to tell us the truth." They heard that "his crown is Torah, *hokhmah* and humility"[18]; his expertise in diverse branches of wisdom made him uniquely able to deal with their question. They assured him that his opinion would be adopted by their community "like the law from Moses on Sinai."

Toward the conclusion of their letter, the rabbis added that this was not their first presentation of this matter to Maimonides. "We have already sent to our Master other letters but we do not know if they reached him." They pleaded that he respond this time and that he send his rejoinder to "Montpellier which is near Narbonne and Marseille … via a trustworthy messenger." It should be addressed to "Rabbi Jonathan, who is one of the [great] rabbis of our land, and one of its righteous ones."

Modern scholars concur that this R. Jonathan of Montpellier was the same R. Jonathan—later, in Lunel—who submitted the twenty-four questions regarding the MT.[19] (In the Lunel letter, R. Jonathan mentioned Maimonides' responsum to them regarding astrology to remind him of his prior association with this group.)[20] Thus, this French community of scholars twice turned to Maimonides with questions of great importance.

What brought them to direct their initial question about astrology to him? The most obvious attraction would have been Maimonides' written works. However, it is clear from their correspondence that his works had not yet reached them. In their letter to Maimonides, they made no reference to his *Commentary on the Mishnah* or the MT. When they lauded his great scholarship, they simply referred to "his books" without even naming one title. Alexander Marx, who discovered and published (1926) the text of the Provencal letter regarding astrology, concluded that Maimonides' "fame … had reached them by rumor rather than his writings."[21] In his response to the scholars, Maimonides himself commented:

> It seems clear that the code which we composed … which I called "*Mishneh Torah* has not reached you. For if it had reached you, you would immediately know my opinion regarding all those matters about which you inquired since we have explained them in … *The Laws of Pagan Worship*…. It seems to me that it will reach you before this responsum since it has already reached the island of Sicily, as it has reached the East [Iraq], the West,[22] and Yemen (Shailat, vol. II, 478).[23]

When the MT reached them—or they sought out a copy themselves—they subjected the work to their learned review. They initiated another correspondence, which is the subject of this study.

The Great Master responded to these various letters from French scholars only after repeated appeals. Despite the urgency of the letter regarding astrology, Maimonides did not respond until 1194 or 1195 (different manuscripts record the date as 11 Tishrei, 4955 or 4956), which was probably a few years after the initial letter (which was undated).[24]

Maimonides' response to the second communication from Provence—the grand letter by R. Jonathan with the twenty-four questions—did not fare any better. This is surprising since this second correspondence demonstrated that the French community, subsequent to its receipt of Maimonides' responsum on astrology, had received Maimonides' works and had mastered those composed in Hebrew, which they could read.[25] Their twenty-four questions demonstrated the high regard they had for his Code. In a cover letter, R. Jonathan also pleaded for a Hebrew translation of his philosophical treatise, *The Guide of the Perplexed*, so that the non-Arabic-speaking Frenchmen could appreciate its wisdom.

One would have thought that Maimonides would have relished the opportunity to defend his MT and to discuss Jewish law with competent scholars who appreciated his Code and expressed great interest in his philosophical work. Yet, no response was issued.

After a period of time, the scholars of Lunel sent a second letter in the name of the entire community rather than under R. Jonathan's signature. Still, no response. They issued another communal appeal. No response. Finally, a fourth letter was sent, this time by R. Jonathan in his own name, appealing for an answer. Right after his signature, he added in tiny letters the following touching personal postscript: "Answer me, our master, pride of Israel, answer me; do not oblige me to ask for help and to shout.... Let it be my lot that I receive a prophetical answer, if it happens while I am still alive...."[26] See Figure 1 on page 25.

After "a few years" (that was Maimonides' phrase; he did not respond until 1199!)[27] the Great Master sent them his response to their twenty-four questions. In a separate letter to the community of Lunel, he sent them the final part of the *Moreh* in the original Arabic—with apologies for his inability to find time to write a translation. In addition to his reply to the Twenty-Four, Maimonides appended a grand *Iggeret*, which is the focus of this study.

I shall offer a translation of this letter in its entirety, followed by a close examination of its content. I will also study the manner in which Maimonides crafted various sources in his formulation of his epistle. My translation is based upon the two standard editions of the *Iggeret*, as found in J. Blau's *Teshuvot ha-Rambam* (*R. Moses b. Maimon—Responsa*),[28] and in Itzhak Shailat's *Iggrot ha-Rambam* (*The Letters and Essays of Moses Maimonides*).[29] Both based their editions on the same manuscripts and both site the extant variants in their footnotes. I tended to rely more on Shailat's work since he had the advantage of following Blau and he discussed Blau's prior contribution. Also, Shailat's notes considered literary and interpretive issues relevant to my work.

The translation of the *Iggeret* was a challenge. Following the norm for epistolary compositions, Maimonides crafted many words or passages to suit his artistic needs. He often did not follow normal grammatical rules. I wished to advance the *Tanakh*-literate reader's pleasure in decoding biblical passages that were the underpinning of many sequences in the *Iggeret*. I endeavored to incorporate in my translations the words used in the Jewish Publication Society's *Tanakh* so that a reader might suspect that a given passage was adapted from Scripture. This occasionally resulted in a less than felicitous translation.

My method of biblical citation also strives to aid the reader in appreciation of Maimonides' craft. Complete or partial *Tanakh* citations are presented within quotation marks, as in the usual manner of text citation. Those passages that Maimonides adapted from the *Tanakh*, modifying the biblical passage to suit his compositional needs, I placed within single quotation marks. Within the citation reference, I will direct the reader to "see" the passage, further indicating that it is an adaptation and not a verbatim quotation. Many of these modified verses will be analyzed in this study. Please note that I have divided the *Iggeret* text into twelve sections. This is my own device to facilitate its analysis. These divisions are not found in the original.

Chapter 1

Maimonides' Grand *Iggeret* to R. Jonathan of Lunel

Unit 1: Welcoming Tribute to R. Jonathan of Lunel

"Who is this coming from Edom in crimson garments from Bozrah? Who is this, majestic in his attire, pressing forward[30] in His great might?" (Is. 63:1). His spirit is "a vigorous spirit" (Ps. 51:14) and his fragrance is like "the fragrance of the fields that the Lord has blessed" (Gen. 27:27). He is girded with his sword and he grasps his weapon to do battle (on behalf of) the Torah but his dwelling place is upon the throne of Talmud. The genial Rabbi, like cool water on a burning hot day, the western pillar who is 'more precious than the finest gold' (see Psalms 19:10), R. Jonathan the Kohen, treasure of the scholars/Kohanim[31], son of our revered Master, Master and Rabbi, David, of blessed memory, may his God be with him for deliverance, "and wherever he [Saul] turned he worsted [them] ..." (I Sam.14:47).

Unit 2: Maimonides' Admiration for R. Jonathan and Prayers for His Well-Being

I—Moses, son of Maimon, of blessed memory—yearn to see you; I delight in your wisdom and rejoice in your fellowship; I pray regularly for the preservation of your tranquility, the abundance of your bounty and for the lengthening of your days.

Unit 3: Scholastic Importance of R. Jonathan and His School

Surely, "you shall be called Priests[32] of the Lord" (Is. 61:6) and you will be found together with 'all who are found inscribed [in the book]' (see Dan. 12:1); you will emerge first among all the valiant within the

Lord's camp, for you are "the Lord's portion" (Deut. 32:9) and 'His allotment' (see Deut. 32:9), who 'yearned after' (see I Samuel 7:2)[33] Him as in former years, who are encamped about his banner (i.e., the Sanctuary), who minister before Him always in his Temple. "Bless, O Lord, his [i.e., the Levite's/priest's] substance" (Deut. 33:11). The Torah scroll was handed down to you, and "from the time the regular offerings is [was] abolished" (Dan. 12:11), it was not abolished from you. All who search for the Lord 'is obedient to your bidding' (see I Sam. 22:14).[34] It was long ago decreed that it is yours to interpret and teach the statutes and the laws; for 'you are the guardians' (see Deut. 33:9) of "the words of the Lord [which] are pure words" (Ps. 12:7)—'guardians of the Covenants' (see Deut. 33:9 and Sotah 37b) as in former years. 'And for whom is all Israel yearning, if not for you and your entire ancestral house?' (see I Sam. 9:20)[35] so that there 'will not be withheld from you a redeemer' (see Ruth 4:14) on behalf of the Torah, as "…was formerly done in Israel…." (Ruth 4:7).

Unit 4: Grand Reception of R. Jonathan's Correspondence by Maimonides and His School

Therefore, when your correspondence [i.e., R. Jonathan's rhymed prose epistle] arrived—filled with all sorts of precious jewels and sapphires, 'enlightening with heavenly radiance those who are wise' (see Dan. 12:3) shining forth with bright light—the students carried it about in their bosom and arms, for with great joy we will hear their wisdom from afar. "As he [Ezra] opened it all the people stood up" (Neh. 8:5). But when its content was revealed, and its hidden secrets were examined, [then] Moses understood and 'he recoiled from it' (see Ex. 4:3). For, together with[in] the correspondence was a letter, hoarding all sorts of precious things [the twenty-four questions, as will become apparent below]. It excelled over all other scrolls because it 'was imbued with a different spirit' (see Num. 14:24)—"a spirit of wisdom and insight; a spirit of counsel and valor" (Is. 11:2).[36] This is the letter which contains the questions and the objections which never had been heard, and the astonishing [questions] which [heretofore] had not been known. A corpulent scholar would 'become lean' (see Is. 17:4) [due to the effort expanded] to comprehend them, and to resolve them he [would have] to ask all seers.

Unit 5: Maimonides' Feigned Astonishment and Enfeeblement at R. Jonathan's Critique of *Mishneh Torah*

So Moses said, "I must turn aside to look at this marvelous sight" (Ex. 3:3). But when he heard the sounds of questions, strong as "a storm wind" (Ps. 107:25 and elsewhere), Moses said, 'this is the sound of the tune of triumph' (see Ex. 32:18). When he saw the high mountains 'he wasn't able to ascend them' (see Ex.19:23). He desired to enter the Tabernacle but the doors were closed. He [R. Jonathan?] 'issued false charges against her' (see Dt. 22:17); he [Maimonides] trembled like those who trembled (see Ex. 19:16). "He pulled back his right hand (Lam. 2:3)" to issue a few words, "but Moses' hands grew heavy" (Ex. 17:12). When he saw that 'neither free nor bond is left' (see Deut. 32:36), he went as he had gone [before] and sat "in a cleft of the rock" (Ex. 33:22). "Moses said to the Lord…. Further, You have said, 'I have singled you out by name, and you have, indeed, gained My favor'" (Ex. 33:12). Yet, in the end, "my children have defeated me" (Talmud, Bava M'zia 59b).

Unit 6: Maimonides' Remarkable and Dramatic Shift from Rhymed to Unadorned Prose

All that has been said [in this letter up to this point is] in a style [literally, "road"] that is not in accordance with my preference—namely, following a road of 'female and male singers' [i.e., poets; see Eccl. 2:8], a partially paved route of figurative terms and similes.[37] This is one of a few [instances] when we have spoken in this fashion or have composed in this manner. [We have done so] since our colleagues and all of our brethren in Sepharad have long followed this road, and our Sages said: "When you enter a city, heed its etiquette" (*Ber. Rabbah* 48:14). However, it is [now] time to return the ocean to its perennial stream so this matter can be appropriately considered.

Unit 7: The Heart of the *Iggeret*: Maimonides' Formal Declaration of His Appreciation for R. Jonathan's Critique and His Identification of His Successor

I, Moses, declare to you—R. Jonathan, Rabbi and Kohen—that when your letters and your questions reached me, I was truly overjoyed on account of them. I said to myself, "Blessed be the Lord, who has not withheld a redeemer from you …." (Ruth 4:14). For I understood that my words had reached someone who understood their content, who comprehended their inner meanings, and who could debate and discuss them appropriately. I said to myself, "He will renew your life and sustain your old age" (Ruth 4:15). All [the questions] you asked, you asked well; all the difficult questions you posed, you posed well. "Fear not, for I am with you" (Is. 43:5).

Unit 8: Maimonides' Apology and Various Explanations for His Tardy Response

I am now sending you[38] a response to each and every one of your questions. The reason why the responses were delayed for a few years was due to my anxiety over my illness and from a multitude of disturbances. I was ill for about a year and although I have now recovered, I am like one who is ill but not in [life-threatening] danger. I remain in bed much of the day. The yoke of responsibility for the health care of the gentiles which is upon my shoulders has dissipated my strength. They do not leave me one free hour, day or night. But what can I do, now my fame has spread in so many lands?

Unit 9: Another Explanation and an Apology for Not Writing His Response in His Own Hand

In addition, I am today not like I was in my youth. My strength has become weak, I am dejected, impatient, my speech is slow, my hands tremble—I tarry even when it comes to writing a brief letter. For this reason, please do not be offended that I arranged for someone else to transcribe my responses [i.e., to the twenty-four questions] and some of my letters[39] [to you]. I did not write everything in my own hand because I didn't have free time for such things because of my weakened physical condition and impatient spirit, and because of all those who burden me at all times.[40]

Unit 10: A Fifth and Final Self-Revealing Explanation: The Competing Claims of Philosophy and Science

And I, Moses, declare to the revered Rabbi, R. Jonathan the Kohen—and to all the scholars and their colleagues who will read my letter—that 'before I was created in the womb the Torah selected me; and before I was born, it consecrated me to its study' (see Jer. 1:5). I was designated 'to cause her springs to gush forth' (see Pr. 5:16). She is my 'loving doe' (see Pr. 5:19), the 'wife of my youth' (see Pr. 5:18); 'my love of her has been my infatuation since my youth' (see Pr. 5:19). Nonetheless, [others, following I Kings 11:1: "many"] "foreign women" became her rival-wives—"Moabite, Ammonite, Edomite, Phoenician, and Hittite women" (I Kings 11:1). God knows that, initially, they were only taken to be her [assistants as] "perfumers, chefs, bakers" (I Sam. 8:13)—"to display her beauty to the peoples and the officials; for she was a[41] beautiful woman" (Est. 1:11). However, her time for sexual congress became diminished (based upon Ex. 21:10) because my heart was divided in to many parts by so many branches of wisdom.

Unit 11: Maimonides' Appraisal of His *Mishneh Torah* as a Comprehensive Code and an Honest Invitation for Critique and Corrections

How I labored—day and night—for some ten consecutive years, putting together this composition. Great men like you will understand what I have done since I brought together things that 'were scattered and dispersed' (see Est. 3:8) between hills and mountains. I called them [together], 'one from a town and two from a clan' (see Jer. 3:14). But, "who can be aware of errors?" (Ps. 19:13) and forgetfulness is a common occurrence for everybody, but even more for the elderly. So for all these reasons it is appropriate to search through my words and to check up after me. A reader of my treatise should not say, "For what will the man be like who will succeed the one who is ruling?" (Eccl. 2:12). Rather, I hereby grant him permission: "'Let him enter,' said the king" (Est. 6:5). You scholars have done me a great favor, and so has anyone else who finds something [in error] and informs me. He has done me a favor so that there will not remain [in the book] any misleading error, Heaven forbid. My intent in this treatise was to clear up the roads and to remove the stumbling blocks from before the students so their minds would not grow weary from the many complicated exchanges [in the Talmud and classical rabbinic texts] which might end in an error in legal decision-making.

Unit 12: A Concluding Prayer on Behalf of R. Jonathan—and on Behalf of Maimonides—for Successful Torah Study

May the Omnipresent, Blessed Be He, assist us and you in [our] study of His Law and in our understanding of His Unity, and may we not stumble.

May the verse be fulfilled in our days and in yours days—"I will put My Teaching into their innermost being and inscribe it upon their hearts" (Jer. 31:33).

Chapter 2

The First Half of the *Iggeret* in Rhymed Prose

The style and language of this text are radically different from what one encounters in Maimonides' philosophical or legal works. Three elements distinguish this composition: rhyme, embellished language, and a unique utilization of biblical verse.[42] In the first half of this text—Units 1 through 5—varying sequences of lines are set in rhyme. This element is unmistakable in the original Hebrew.

Second, Maimonides crafted this part of his epistle in artistically fashioned language, rich with metaphors and embellished terminologies in a fashion that distinguishes it from his usual rhetorical style. I shall discuss this phenomenon below.

Finally, Maimonides incorporated biblical verses into his epistle in a distinctive fashion. As any reader of rabbinic writings can attest, biblical passages are quoted in all genres and periods. The various midrashim, Mishna, Talmud, rabbinic commentary, jurisprudence, or correspondence, regularly cite biblical passages as proof-texts to support a law, argument, or teaching. Such quotes are usually identified by a header and the source is often cited. ("As it is written in ….") These citations are identified thereby as independent of the composition.

In much of Maimonides' rhymed prose epistle, biblical texts became the language of the *Iggeret*. He embedded biblical verses—in full or in part—into his letter without a distinguishing reference. If the passage did not fit within the rhetoric of the letter, Maimonides altered its gender, number, referent, etc., so that it melded into his text.

In the translation of the *Iggeret* presented above, each biblical or Midrashic passage or adaptation was identified with quotation marks and its source was provided. Although this might be helpful to the reader of this study, this identification undoes an important aspect of this genre of composition, which was the joy of discovery of biblical/Midrashic citations embedded within the text. Since these passages were not identified by Maimonides as quotations, they would emerge as delightful surprises to a reader who was *Tanakh*-literate and would recognize and appreciate Maimonides' artistic creation. He displayed great artistry and apparent ease in this undertaking.[43]

Dan Pagis, discussing the distinctive conventions of Hebrew poetry of the Late Middle Ages, stated:

> Hebrew poetry used not only biblical vocabulary but also biblical idioms or verses which were interwoven into the fabric of the poem among other ornaments of style. This ... was not a mechanical mosaic of quotations, but a peculiar and original combination in a new context, which often led to a surprising change in meaning whose effect sometimes was humorous.[44]

In this letter of fifty-nine printed lines (in Blau's edition), there are twenty-seven unaltered quotations of biblical passages (in full or in part) and twenty-eight adaptations. Box 1 records these occurrences; an asterisk indicates an adaptation. Maimonides used passages from a wide range of biblical books. Some of the unusual and/or interesting citations or adaptations will be discussed below.

Box 1. *Tanakh* Citations/Adaptations in Maimonides' *Iggeret*

1. Isaiah 63:1
2. Psalms 51:14
3. Genesis 27:27
4. Psalms 19:10*
5. I Samuel 14:47
6. Isaiah 61:6
7. Daniel 12:1*
8. Deuteronomy 32:9*
9. Deuteronomy 32:9*
10. I Samuel 7:2*
11. Deuteronomy 33:11
12. Daniel 12:11
13. I Samuel 22:14*
14. Deuteronomy 33:9
15. Psalms 12:7
16. Deuteronomy 33:9*
17. I Samuel 9:20*
18. Ruth 4:14*
19. Ruth 4:7
20. Daniel 12:3*
21. Nehemiah 8:5
22. Exodus 4:3*
23. Numbers 14:24*
24. Isaiah 11:2
25. Isaiah 17:4*
26. Exodus 3:3

27. Psalms 107:25
28. Exodus 32:18*
29. Exodus 19:23*
30. Deuteronomy 22:17*
31. Exodus 19:16*
32. Lamentations 2:3
33. Exodus 17:12
34. Deuteronomy 32:36*
35. Exodus 33:22
36. Exodus 33:12
(The rhymed prose section of the *Iggeret* concludes at this point.)
37. Ecclesiastes 2:8*
38. Ruth 4:14
39. Ruth 4:15
40. Isaiah 43:5
41. Jeremiah 1:5*
42. Proverbs 5:16*
43. Proverbs 5:19*
44. Proverbs 5:18*
45. Proverbs 5:19*
46. I Kings 11:1*
47. I Samuel 8:13
48. Esther 1:11
49. Exodus 21:10*
50. Esther 3:8*
51. Jeremiah 3:14*
52. Psalms 19:13
53. Ecclesiastes 2:12
54. Esther 6:5
55. Jeremiah 31:33

Maimonides used a biblical verse (Is. 63:1) to open his epistle with a dramatic flourish. With this passage, he feigned astonishment at the unanticipated arrival of a scholarly challenge to his MT: "Who is this coming from Edom in crimson garments from Bozrah…? … girded with his sword … to do battle." But right after he recorded his surprise at this sudden attack, he proceeded to heap generous praises upon R. Jonathan and the Lunel scholars. He depicted R. Jonathan as a noble and worthy opponent, possessing "great might … Lord has blessed … his dwelling place is upon the throne of Talmud. The genial Rabbi, like cool water on a burning hot day, the western pillar who is more precious than the finest gold." He lauded R. Jonathan the "treasure of the scholars" and revered his father: "son of our revered Master, Master and Rabbi, David, of blessed memory."

He complimented R. Jonathan's students: "Surely, you shall be called Priests of the Lord" (Is. 61:6). Throughout his letter, he gushed with exaggerated tributes to his correspondents and their questions.

Given the relationship between Maimonides and the Lunel scholars that I presented earlier, we know that Maimonides did not know his Lunel interlocutors. Although he will acknowledge (Unit 7) that their twenty-four questions demonstrated their mastery of Talmudic law, these exaggerated tributes and compliments were driven largely by the genre of epistolary composition, which mandated such rhetoric.

In a forthcoming book, *Dominion Built of Praise: Panegyric and Legitimacy among Jews in the Medieval Mediterranean*, Jonathan Decter examines the culture of praise which, derived largely from Arabic poetics, had influenced Jewish literary expression. He traces a compositional style spanning many cultures, which often entailed, according to S. D. Goitein, "exasperating ... hyperbolic generalities."[45] A seventeenth-century dictionary defined panegyrics as "a licentious kind of speaking ... in the praise and commendation of Kings, or other great persons, wherein some falsities are joined with many flatteries."[46] Decter states: "Panegyrics were exchanged between confidants who knew each other intimately but also between individuals residing at vast distances who knew each other by reputation only."[47] He comments that such poetry often contained "tropes that were ... predictable" and "seldom offered any personal data that a biographer or historian might find of interest."[48] He reflects that praise "helped bind [these individuals] within a specific social and intellectual circle,"[49] which certainly justified Maimonides' remarks in his letter to the Lunel scholars. I will later identify some of the sources for Maimonides' effusive compliments to the Lunel scholars.

The opening of the *Iggeret* and many of its elements reflected the norm for this genre. He composed his epistle in panegyric style—that is, he used exaggerated language to compliment the Lunel scholars—and contemporary readers would have read these passages accordingly. This placed Maimonides in a difficult position. In this instance, the author of these lines truly regarded his correspondents as men of admirable scholarship. Although Maimonides used language that was mandated and formulaic, he actually regarded the Lunel circle highly as worthy masters of Torah. This necessitated an unusual turn within the *Iggeret*, which will be analyzed below.

These opening praises may have been formulaic. However, Maimonides did know the country of his correspondents. In light of this, Maimonides' choice to open with the Isaiah passage was much more than an artistic device. By identifying the warrior as "coming from Edom," Maimonides set up the cultural context of this correspondence. In Midrashic texts, the rabbis identified Rome as a descendent of Edom, and Edom became a code word for the countries and cultures of Christian Europe.[50] In a responsum to Tyre, Maimonides referred his (unidentified) correspondent to his *Sefer Hamitzvot* [*Book on the Commandments*] which, he observed, had already reached "the Edomite countries," by which he meant the western Christian nations.[51] By connecting R. Jonathan with Edom, Maimonides cast this correspondence as an encounter between the scholars of Christian Europe and Moses ben Maimon, "the Sephardi." (Similarly, Maimonides' tribute to R. Jonathan as "the western pillar" alluded to his location.)

In Unit 3, Maimonides heaped great praise upon the members of the school of R. Jonathan by identifying them as recipients of the Torah and "guardians of the Covenants." Maimonides also stated that all the men in this circle were "called priests" who "minister before Him." They had the noble responsibility "to interpret and teach the statutes and the laws," like the Kohanim (of the priestly clan of biblical Aaron) of ancient Israel.[52]

In fact, the only Lunel individual identified in this correspondence was the leader, R. Jonathan, and he was a Kohen. Maimonides, however, elevated the entire group to share his priestly status.

Decter illustrates how Jews borrowed many rhetorical conventions from Arab writings, and they are well attested in Maimonides' *Iggeret*. He notes that in Islamic civilization, "Letter writing became an art form in its own right that merited the composition of manuals offering advice for scribes...."[53] He states that these manuals "not only reflect the aesthetic and intellectual ideals of the age but also reveal a great deal about how society was organized and how the relations among various ranks of people were imagined."[54] Maimonides' reference to the Lunel scholars as priests who teach and minister to their flock would have been received by the Lunel group as an honored tribute.

In Unit 4, Maimonides shifted his focus from the authors of the correspondence to their letters. It opens with Maimonides' declaration of his joy and excitement upon receipt of the Lunel correspondence "filled with all sorts of precious jewels ... enlightening with heavenly radiance...." Its contents were eagerly anticipated as "wisdom from afar." But that joy was quickly dashed when the full correspondence was read. Maimonides noted the appearance of "questions and objections which had not been heard." When the entire set of letters was read, Moses, the son of Maimon, "recoiled from it" (see Ex. 4:3).

This unit contains two stylistic devices that also appear in other writings of Maimonides, as will be illustrated below. In the first device, an object or persona previously perceived as benevolent is suddenly viewed in a negative fashion. R. Jonathan's epistle, which was initially received enthusiastically and joyfully, is subsequently perceived as a threat. Such reversal or conversion will be discussed at length below.

The second device was Maimonides' application to himself of terminologies, images, and events about the biblical Moses. Units 4 and 5 are full of biblical passages—in full or adapted fashion—which dealt with Moses' life, persona, or career. Many reflect his difficult role as transmitter of the law to the people of Israel.

Maimonides first used this device to convey his reaction to the discovery that the Lunel correspondence challenged his MT: "But when it [i.e., the full correspondence from R. Jonathan] was read and its content revealed, its hidden secrets examined, [then] Moses understood and 'he recoiled from it.'" The phrase was adapted from the fourth chapter of Exodus, which dealt with the commissioning of Moses. Despite God's insistence that Moses serve as leader to the Israelites, Moses resists the divine call. Finally,

> The Lord said to him, "What is that in your hand?" And he replied, "A rod."
> He said, "Cast it on the ground." He cast it on the ground and it became a snake; and Moses recoiled from it (verses 2–3).

The rod that shepherd Moses carried to lead his flock—and which he will use to convince both Egyptians and fellow Israelites of his leadership—was converted by the Lord to something awesome and frightening. It became an object that convinced Moses to adhere to God's call.

Maimonides appropriated that passage to portray his shock at the correspondence from R. Jonathan. He fashioned an analogy between the life events of his biblical namesake and his situation vis-à-vis the Lunel scholars. Throughout Unit 5, he invoked that comparison.

He mimicked Moses, who declared, upon observing a burning bush from afar, "I must turn aside to look at this marvelous sight" (Ex. 3:3). Maimonides used that expression to express his eagerness to study and appreciate the epistle that R. Jonathan had sent him. But when he completed this examination, he compared his reaction to Moses, who "wasn't able to ascend" (see Ex. 19:23) the mountain and whose "hands grew heavy" (Ex. 17:12). The phrase "but Moses' hands grew heavy" was stated when Moses could no longer maintain upraised hands by which the warring Amalekites could be defeated.

When Maimonides examined R. Jonathan's correspondence more closely, he repeated Moses' woeful exclamation from the top of Mt. Sinai that he heard "the tune of triumph" (see Ex. 32:18) chanted by the Israelites below. That passage introduces a theme that Maimonides will develop in the epistle and that will serve as the finale of this unit. He feared—like Moses—that his teachings might be rejected by their recipients. He paralleled the near-rejection of God's teachings by ancient Israel with the Provencal attempt to "defeat" his MT.

One passage in Unit 5 is especially difficult. Maimonides wrote:

'He issued false charges against her'; he trembled like those who trembled.

The antecedents in both passages are indefinite: who issued the false charges and who trembled? The first line uses terminologies found in Deuteronomy 22:17, in which a father claimed that his new son-in-law had issued "false charges" against his daughter, the bride. R. Itzhak Shailat, in his commentary to Maimonides' epistle, suggested two possible interpretations: "This could be interpreted in reference to R. Jonathan: that it was he who issued 'false charges'—difficult challenges—against the *Hibbur* (the 'daughter' of Maimonides). It is also possible to interpret that it referred to Maimonides, who started to present 'claims'; that is, to consider possible rejoinders to the challenges of the letter [i.e., the twenty-four of R. Jonathan]."[55]

The first interpretation seems more convincing but suffers from the fact that it changes the subject of the verb from Maimonides and his reaction to the twenty-four to R. Jonathan.

The source for the second passage—"He trembled like those who trembled"—and its meaning are even more obscure. Maimonides might have crafted it upon a word in Exodus 19:16b: "and all the people who were in the camp trembled." This verse referred to the awesome anticipation of the Israelites prior to the revelation at Mt. Sinai. While Moses ascended the mountain, the people below shuddered with great fear, as the Theophany was about to occur.

Maimonides may have used that passage to declare that, upon hearing the twenty-four questions—the "revelations" of R. Jonathan—he trembled like the ancient Israelites in reaction to the divine Revelation. The implied comparison between the *Mishneh Torah* and Torah is artistically imaginative. These images are especially powerful because they seem—to modern sensitivities—to be shockingly impious.

The last two appropriations of Mosaic passages were even more daring. The first was constructed upon a difficult biblical verse in Deuteronomy:

> When he saw that 'neither free nor bond is left' (see Deut. 32:36),[56] he went as he had gone [before] and sat "in a cleft of the rock" (Ex. 33:22). "And Moses said to the Lord.... Further, You have said, 'I have singled you out by name, and you have, indeed, gained My favor'" (Ex. 33:12).

The precise meaning of 'neither free nor bond is left' is unclear.[57] The entire verse in Deuteronomy may mean that when Israel's plight had become desperate and they recognized that the pagan gods they had relied upon could not save them, God would deliver them. Only when no other option was available, would God intercede.

In the next passage, Maimonides developed selections of Exodus 33. After the sin of the Golden Calf, the future of the Jewish people hung in the balance: would they be able to reconcile with God? Moses entreated with God and reminded Him that He had chosen Moses ("I have singled you out by name"—Ex. 33:12) and vouchsafed his protection (ibid.). In this desperate moment he challenged God to demonstrate His allegiance to His people: "For how shall it be known that Your people have gained Your favor unless You go with us..." (v. 16).

Maimonides, portraying himself as one who had been defeated by his Provencal critics, adopted Moses' plea to God to redeem him from ignominy. He appropriated passages from one of the most sublime moments of Moses' career as his petition for divine intervention on behalf of his MT. Maimonides made a gargantuan leap: he applied Moses' desperate petition for divine salvation of the entire Israelite nation to his own scholarly debate with the Provencal scholars.

Maimonides concluded this unit with a complaint by God Himself regarding His people of Israel: "Yet, in the end, 'my children have defeated me.'" This phrase was excerpted from a midrash cited in the Talmud (Bava M'zia 59b), which described a debate between scholars regarding a particular point of Halakhah. In the context of this discussion, one scholar invoked various miracles to reveal God's opinion on this matter. Although one would have thought that such proof would be decisive, the rabbis responded that God's Torah was no longer in heaven, and majority rule as defined by mortals would determine Halakhah. Later in that discussion, the Talmud asked what God was doing when that decision was taken that excluded Him from a role in the administration of His Law. Elijah the prophet advised

R. Nathan that "He smiled and said, 'My children have defeated me, my children have defeated me.'" Maimonides excerpted that divine exclamation to mark the end of the rhymed prose section of his epistle.

This was Maimonides' most daring textual adaptation. In the numerous applications of Mosaic passages to Maimonides' own situation that were discussed above, the Grand Rabbi demonstrated his artistic finesse and a great flair for unanticipated metaphors. The reader would derive much pleasure upon discovery of the original biblical context of these passages. With his finale, Maimonides took a more daring—possibly irreverent—step by using a "divine utterance" as his own declaration. True, the words cited were excerpted from a Midrash and not Holy Writ; however, the impact was the same. He positioned himself to be in the same relationship vis-à-vis his Provencal disputants as the Almighty was to the Talmudic rabbis. Just as divine wisdom could be superseded by human judgment, so too could Maimonides' teachings be incorrectly repudiated. His *Mishneh Torah* could be rejected by the Lunel rabbis just as God's word had been overridden by the Talmudic rabbis.

As his finale for the first part of his *Iggeret*, Maimonides echoed the Almighty's declaration of rejection: "My children have defeated me!"

The above analysis illustrates that Maimonides composed his epistle in accordance with the literary conventions of the era. In a milieu of literate and cultured societies, prosperity, and cultural and religious tolerance, a new form of poetic expression developed in Jewish circles that was greatly influenced by Arab literary principles and models.[58] Scholars of medieval Hebrew literature have demonstrated that "the imitation of Arabic metrics by Hebrew poets was a conscious and intentional act…."[59] Two centuries before Maimonides, a new literary style developed in Muslim Spain—especially in Andalusia—and subsequently in Christian Spain and Provence. The form of rhymed prose in which the *Iggeret* was written is well attested during the age of Maimonides, with compositions going back to the eleventh century and examples of this genre in the Cairo Geniza as well.

Chapter 3

Maimonides' Unanticipated and Problematic Style Reversal

The style of Maimonides' rhymed prose *Iggeret* differed substantially from his other works. I cited above (p. xiii) his comments within his *Commentary to the Mishnah* (Hagigah 3:2) where he enjoined his readers to "...examine carefully our words.... And do not read them hastily and superficially; rather, read them thoroughly and with careful reflection."

In his Introduction to the MT, he emphasized how he strove to make his work readily accessible to his readers—young and old, educated and not. He wrote that he endeavored to use language that was "clear and concise" so that his code could be easily comprehended.[60]

Isadore Twersky observed: "Time and again, Maimonides emphasized the precision and meticulousness of his writing. Everything is deliberate and exact; each idea is formulated with great care, every juxtaposition of distinct subjects is calculated, every sentence is written with due consideration.... Nothing was written by chance, by inadvertence, or solely for rhetorical effect."[61]

Maimonides' compositional goals could not be sustained in a rhymed prose epistle in which rhetorical effect was an essential and defining element. Decter notes that "many panegyric texts functioned essentially as letters or as part of a correspondence in which a poem accompanied a letter proper, itself often written in rhymed prose with extensive literary effects."[62] Maimonides' *Iggeret* was such a composition. In his epistle to his Lunel correspondents, Maimonides donned a poetic mantle that required him to cast aside his usual compositional trappings.

Maimonides himself acknowledged this departure in an unusual passage in the *Iggeret*. In Unit 6, he openly announced that the style in which he had written thus far was not his own preference, and that he had adopted it as a necessary concession to Sephardic literary convention:

> All that has been said [in this letter up to this point is] in a style [literally, "road"] that is not in accordance with my preference—namely, following a road of "female and male singers" [i.e., poets; see Eccl. 2:8], a partially paved route of figurative terms and similes. This is one of a few [instances] when we have spoken in this fashion or have composed in this manner. [We have done so] since our colleagues and all of our brethren in Sepharad have long followed this road, and our Sages said: "When you enter a city, heed its etiquette" (*Ber. Rabbah* 48:14). However, it is [now] time to return the ocean to its perennial stream so this matter can be appropriately considered.

In this passage, Maimonides opined that Provencal literary norms "followed this road" of "Sepharad." Indeed, R. Jonathan had sent him two rhymed prose epistles, both of which were composed in accordance with the conventional norms for the genre. With surprising candor, Maimonides remarked that his *Iggeret* was written in rhymed prose to comply with the expected literary/social norms. In truth, he stated, he would have preferred to have followed the "perennial stream" to which he then returned for the remainder of his epistle.

We can only wonder how Maimonides' disparaging remarks about his *Iggeret* were received by his Provencal correspondents. Since R. Jonathan's two letters demonstrated that the Lunel scholars considered such compositions to be necessary elements within a correspondence between honored colleagues, Maimonides' remarks could have been received as impolitic. Authors usually do not compose an important letter to a respected recipient that they send together with an apology for its style.

Possibly, Maimonides' announcement of style reversal—"This is one of a few [instances] when we have spoken in this fashion or have composed in this manner"—was to be taken literally. We have compositions from this period written by professional scribes/poets, who developed a text for individuals who were unable to compose a proper epistle. (See Appendix, which discusses a letter composed by Judah Halevi on behalf of R. Joseph Ibn Migas.) Such compositions demonstrate that, if a correspondent was unable to compose a proper epistle, he would hire a professional writer to do so.

Maimonides' apology/explanation in his *Iggeret* might reflect this convention. Since he felt he did not have appropriate skills, he should have engaged someone to present a proper epistle to his honored Lunel correspondents. In this instance, he announced, he decided to revert back to a style with which he was more familiar.

Maimonides might have curtailed his rhymed prose composition for an additional reason, which was his negative attitude toward poetry in general. Throughout his writings during all periods of his life, Maimonides spoke critically of poetic compositions. (See Appendix for a review of those statements.) His disparaging remarks here regarding rhymed prose might also have been stimulated by his overall attitude toward poetry.[63]

I don't think any of these deterrents—lack of training and experience, his compositional guidelines, or his attitude toward poetry—was the driving force behind his reversal. Given the dominance of this genre in the Spain of his youth, it is inconceivable that he was not tutored in its style. Graetz stated regarding twelfth-century Spain that "…this period was rich in poets…. The Arabic custom of writing letters of friendship in verses, adopted by the Spanish Jews, made … knowledge of prosody a necessity: he who did not desire to appear illiterate had to learn how to versify. The number of poems which at this period saw the light of day was legion."[64] Since this genre had spread throughout the Arabic-speaking world, it was unlikely that Maimonides was unschooled in this manner of writing.

In addition to the ubiquity of these compositions, the structure of Maimonides' epistle and its language displayed confident competence with the genre as well as mastery and creative skill with its registers. The form and substance of his *Iggeret* belied a protestation of innocence: it does not read like a maiden voyage in the poetic streams of Spanish-style Hebrew poetry. For these reasons, I found his announced style reversal problematic, and sought to find a justification driven by more substantial motivations.

As of this juncture, I have examined only the first section of the epistle. I will later subject the second part of Maimonides' epistle to a thorough textual review. My interpretation of that segment, together with other letters, will justify the style reversal on solid Maimonidean ground. However, before undertaking that analysis, I wish to explore other texts that illustrate Maimonides' involvement in poetical composition *a la Sepharad*. I found ample evidence that the Great Master was no stranger to the contemporary poetic genre.

Jacob Mann discovered a letter in the Cairo Geniza that he thought might have been addressed to Maimonides.[65] This letter of seventeen lines was written in elegant Hebrew; however, the first three lines of the document, which probably contained the name of the addressee, were missing. The letter was composed by an Al-Fayyumi ben Sa'adya to a "Moreh Tzedek" (honorable/just Judge). The writer lauded his recipient's legal expertise and his honored position in the community: "I rejoice, am overjoyed and bow down before the Creator of all, who has placed within His people such a blessing…."

Al-Fayyumi apologized for the brevity of his letter due to being pressed for time but he explained that he wrote "with the intent not to allow the friendship to dissolve." Apparently, the sole purpose of his brief note was to maintain a connection with the recipient. He concluded with prayers for his welfare and "the welfare of his precious one, his family and friends, and all those associated with him."

This was a letter to a highly regarded communal leader from someone eager to preserve an association or friendship with him. Mann considered it likely that it was addressed to Maimonides. If that attribution is correct, the reference to "his precious one"—which surely meant a much beloved son—would provide an overall date for the letter. Maimonides was almost fifty when his son, Abraham, was born in 1186.[66] By that time, Maimonides had already composed his *Commentary on the Mishnah*, *Book on the Commandments*, and the MT. His position of leadership within the local Jewish community and beyond was well established, as was his role as a physician. In the opening salvo of compliments to his recipient, Al-Fayyumi complimented this "Moreh Tzedek" not only for his role as a just and revered teacher of the Law, but as a gifted composer of many "beautiful poems ('shirim'), elegant and proper; I examined them all and, indeed, they are beautiful and comely."

Mann remarks:

> The writer flatters his correspondent as the author of "beautiful poems," but we know that Maimonides' fame was not due to his achievements in this branch of literature. As was the fashion of the time, he would compose his Hebrew letters in rhymed prose. An admirer might have regarded them as poetry. But the sage's whole bent lay in a direction quite removed from the imaginative flights of the muse.[67]

Mann correctly noted that the compliment here is for beautiful poetry, not rhymed prose, which was more widely practiced. Although Mann reflected in his footnotes to this selection[68] that we do have other compositions by Maimonides, he remarked that the Great Master's fame was not for his poetic creations.

If Maimonides was the "Moreh Tzedek" of this letter, it provides evidence that the Great Master was not only a gifted composer of rhymed prose but of "beautiful poems," which probably meant poetry in its usual form. Although this source is not definitive, if its referent was Maimonides, we have testimony that the poetic muse was no stranger to the Great Master.

Chapter 4

Maimonides' Letter to Judge Anatoli

In fact, we have another epistle composed by Maimonides in rhymed prose. It was written to a R. Anatoli ben Joseph, who emigrated from Provence to Egypt and accepted an appointment to serve as judge in Alexandria.[69] R. Anatoli turned to Maimonides with various questions. Neither his questions nor Maimonides' responses have survived, but we do have epistles that they exchanged with each other in conjunction with their halakhic correspondence. Like the *Iggeret* to R. Jonathan, it was written in Hebrew since this Frenchman did not know Arabic. Neither of their epistles was dated; however, since R. Anatoli referred to Maimonides' *Guide*, which was composed around 1191, his correspondence with Maimonides probably occurred shortly after he arrived in Egypt in the early 1190s. Even if Maimonides did not reply "for a few years," as was his custom during that exceedingly demanding period of his life, it would mean that his response to R. Anatoli was probably written a few years before his letter to R. Jonathan of Lunel.

This letter was an independent rhymed prose composition of fifty-eight lines. Many literary devices, terms, phrases, and biblical verses found in this text are also found in the letter to Lunel. It also contained the same structural elements as the letter to R. Jonathan, although the order of these sections was shifted in accordance with its purpose.

In this letter, Maimonides described the arrival of a letter "laden with precious stones" that he admired. "When I took it from the carrier I wasn't sure to whom it was sent and who the sender was." He heaped praises upon the letter, citing or adapting phrases from *Song of Songs*, in which the lover likened his beloved to a "closed garden" or "sealed spring," suggesting that her hidden charms would ultimately produce beneficial fruits. He delighted in the beauty of his sudden visitor: "A crown of kingship is on her head."

In the next section, a reversal took place when the unanticipated visitor displayed an unexpected threatening or challenging aspect.[70] He "observed that... [although] her glory is awesome....Her piercing eyes are arrows ready to shoot at her admirers...." "I trembled and was frightened. I said to her, 'my daughter.... Turn your eyes from me.... My glory had turned to a destructive agent.... Place a veil upon yourself....'"

Maimonides used a unique term for "veil"—"masveh"—which appears in only one place in the Bible. Exodus 34:29–35 states that Moses' face would become radiant when God spoke to him. When these rays surrounded his face, Aaron and the Israelites feared to approach him. In order to allow the Israelites to approach him, Moses placed a "veil"—"masveh"—upon his face (verse 33). With wonderful artistry, Moses, the son of Maimon, asked his surprise visitor to protect him by placing on her face a "masveh." Unlike the biblical Moses, who wore a "masveh" to protect others from his radiance, the latter-day Moses sought protection from a similar veil worn by his namesake. As in his letter to R. Jonathan, Maimonides creatively adapted to himself images or passages about Moses. His delightful use of this unique biblical term was medieval Hebrew poetics at its best.

In the next unit, Maimonides depicted the letter as a maiden. "I then asked her, saying: 'Whose daughter are you?'" She responded that she was the daughter of a great man in Israel who grew up in the tents of learning. He is well trained in the art of battling to defend the Torah, she responded, which was the same imagery Maimonides used regarding R. Jonathan (*Iggeret* Unit 1).

The daughter then lavished praise and honor on her father, declaring that he had contributed much to implant Torah scholarship and enlightenment. She announced his name—Anatoli—and that he was en route, "and merely to see your face would be his reward; [therefore] he has sent before him Rachel, his daughter.... If it pleases you to attend to the matters [about which I will speak] ... otherwise, if it does not please you, I will return, with embittered spirit ... to my family and the house of my father." Maimonides responded: "I will redeem you...." He then used phrases from *Ruth* urging the maiden "don't go elsewhere" and "...stay here close to my girls" (Ruth 2:8).

The next unit is a complicated metaphor of intricately developed biblical phrases containing the message Maimonides wanted to convey: although the maiden's father could claim a substantial dowry given her beauty—i.e., R. Anatoli's important questions warranted a proper response—that could occur only in due time. One again, the objective of Maimonides' letter was to convey his apology for a tardy response. In order to sweeten this message, Maimonides wrote that he "rejoiced at your composition like one who has found a treasure-trove." He compared his joy at this correspondence to refreshing dew "on a burning hot day," and he stated that R. Anatoli reflected "the fragrance of the fields that the Lord has blessed (Gen. 27:27)." Maimonides had used the same terminologies in his letter to R. Jonathan (*Iggeret* Unit 1) in which he referred to refreshing water "on a burning hot day" and also cited Genesis 27:27. He assured R. Anatoli that "All have rejoiced at your coming to our land" and concluded with conventional prayers for his welfare: he petitioned that God will enable him to influence and lead with tranquility, and that he not falter or err in his judgments.

The objectives of Maimonides' letter were twofold: (1) to acknowledge receipt of R. Anatoli's questions and to record his high regard for them and for their author; and (2) to advise him that he could not deal with them at present but his delay should not be mistakenly perceived as a reflection of Maimonides' disregard for him or his correspondence. The main purpose of the letter was to justify Maimonides' delayed response and to offer, in advance, an apology. When we compare Maimonides' letter to R. Jonathan with his epistle to R. Anatoli, the similarity is obvious.

Given the many common features shared by these epistles—language, biblical citations, images, motives, and themes—it is possible that Maimonides' letter to Judge Anatoli served as a prototype for the *Iggeret* to R. Jonathan. Given the enormous medical demands on his time in the late 1190s,[71] he might have decided to compose his reply to the Lunel circle drawing upon the structure and rhetoric of a letter he had written previously for another Provencal scholar.

There is another explanation for the similarities between these epistles. Possibly, these common features were popular elements used by many authors of rhymed prose epistles. I will discuss this below.

Chapter 5

The Letters from R. Jonathan of Lunel

We cannot prove that Maimonides fashioned his Lunel epistle deliberately following his prior letter to R. Anatoli. The next two sources, however, had an unquestionable influence upon the epistle Maimonides wrote to Lunel: the two letters he received from R. Jonathan. The first accompanied the twenty-four questions; the second was written after no response was received either to R. Jonathan's initial letter or to the two letters from the entire Lunel community. These texts were obviously in Maimonides' hands when he fashioned his Lunel *Iggeret*; they were the stimuli for his rhymed prose composition. Had the Lunel scholars simply sent out the twenty-four questions without a literary accompaniment, Maimonides would have responded by addressing the substance of their enquiry directly, as he did in his other responsa. Since the Lunel group drafted an epistle "following a road of 'female and male singers,' a partially paved route of figurative terms and similes" (Unit 6), he was motivated to respond in kind.

What is the textual relationship of these two epistles to Maimonides' rejoinder? Do they share similar content, themes, and terminologies?

The second letter has a treasured provenance.[72] This text was found in the Cairo Geniza, and scholars have concluded that this document is the original letter, written in R. Jonathan's own hand (Figure 1).[73] It also contains writing from Maimonides. On the back of the vellum page is a note (in Arabic and partially distorted) which Maimonides wrote to remind himself about the contents and purpose of this correspondence and the need to respond to its various requests.[74] This autograph is a rich and moving piece of literary history. It ultimately was acquired by the Bodleian Library and is the subject of scholarly articles by S. M. Stern, who also translated the epistle.[75]

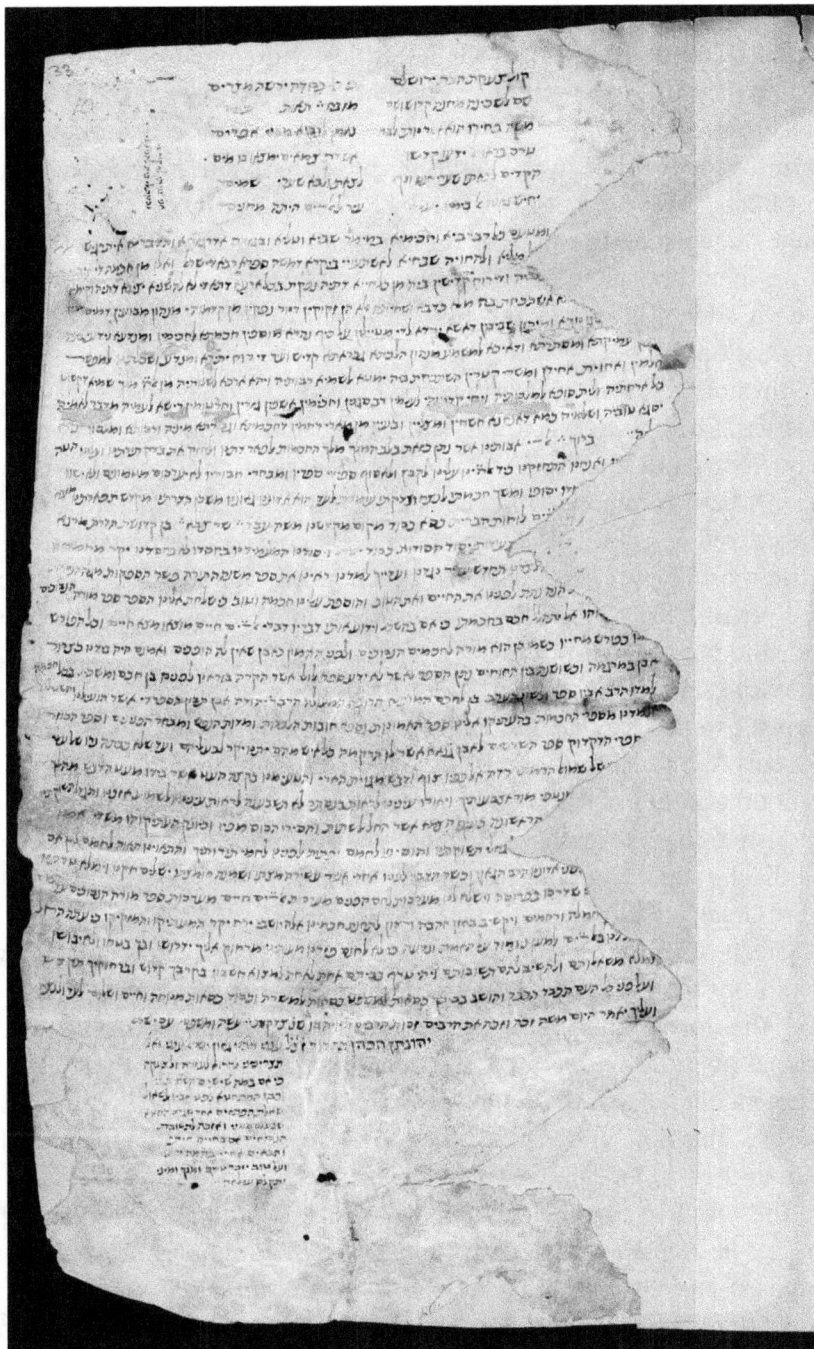

Figure 1: R. Jonathan's second letter; Bodleian Library, Genizah Fragments, MS. Heb. b. 11/32, folio 33a.

Above the actual body of the letter is a six-line poem written in two parallel columns. The text of the letter below the poem is in two parts. The first nine lines are written in Aramaic followed by twenty-three lines in Hebrew. Above and below the body of the letter are two notes written in tiny letters but in the same script as the main body of the letter. Most likely, these are notes written by R. Jonathan himself after he completed the epistle. The note at the bottom—cited above (p. xvii)—was his personal appeal to Maimonides that he respond "while I am still alive." It adds a dramatic and human touch to this formal and elegant composition.

The note at the top was written at a right angle to the text of the body of the letter. It was placed vertically, running up and down, on the left side of the poem that preceded the Aramaic lines. This postscript states, in rhymed prose: "I have commanded my consecrated one to build for him a house, to be offered as a present." Stern offers the following interpretation: "This means, most likely: I have asked a friend of mine, a good poet, to compose these verses ["bayit," literally, a "house," meaning a verse]; Jonathan evidently did not aspire himself to poetical laurels."[76]

With remarkable honesty, R. Jonathan appended a note at the top of his epistle to declare that although it was necessary for him to render "his great correspondent the courtesy of writing the letter in his own hand," he was not the author of the poem that preceded it. Although R. Jonathan was obviously trained to write in rhymed prose, he apparently was not confidant that he could compose a poem that would properly convey his respect for the Great Seer of Egypt.[77]

Given Maimonides' non-responsiveness to his first letter and the two letters from the Lunel community, R. Jonathan may have decided to pull out all the stops in this fourth communication. Not only did he hire a professional poet, he posted a conspicuous note at the top of the epistle to document the efforts the Lunel community made to earn Maimonides' response. This note underscored the great esteem that R. Jonathan had for Maimonides.

The first letter from R. Jonathan—which Prof. Blau included in his *Teshuvot ha-Rambam*, placing it right before Maimonides' *Iggeret*[78]—was composed entirely in complex Hebrew rhymed prose. It contained 128 printed lines (in Blau's edition)—twice as long as Maimonides' fifty-nine-line epistle—and it featured rhyme, elegant language, and the utilization of biblical passages and Midrashic texts as its medium of expression.

The epistle opened with a dramatic charge to its carrier: "Rush this scroll to the house of our Master...." The first line conveyed the urgency and importance of this correspondence to its Provencal authors. Given their modest connection with the Sage of Egypt, these men needed to use all means at their disposal to solicit a response, including flattery. The panegyric style is readily apparent in Jonathan's letter: Maimonides, known only by reputation, is called "our Master," and elevated language is replete in the epistle.

Maimonides' dramatic opening of his *Iggeret*—"Who is this coming from Edom in crimson garments from Bozrah? Who is this, majestic in his attire, pressing forward in His great might?" (Is. 63:1)—could be read as his response to R. Jonathan. In his letter, R. Jonathan ordered the speedy delivery of the epistle; Maimonides reacted—"What is this unsolicited communication which has so suddenly appeared at my door?"

A few lines into his letter, R. Jonathan presented a delightful adaptation of Isaiah 59:19. The original stated, "From the west, they shall revere the name of the Lord, And from the east, His Presence." The passage reflected the worldwide homage to the Almighty. R. Jonathan made two textual changes to this verse to redirect its homage from God to Maimonides. He wrote: "From the west, they shall revere his name, and from the east, his presence." In the first half of the passage, he substituted "his name" for "the name of the Lord" and, in the second half, he changed "His Presence" to "his presence." This is the first of many instances in which R. Jonathan applied to Maimonides a biblical passage that, in the original, referred to God, Moses, or other biblical figures.

R. Jonathan also used the Isaiah passage to set up an East-West context for this correspondence. His line—"From the west, they shall revere his name..."—established their respective cultural milieux. As I observed above (p. 1 and pp. 10–11), Maimonides opened his *Iggeret* by identifying the newly arrived letter with Edom. The openings of both letters contained similar elements.

In the first few lines of the letter, R. Jonathan cited Isaiah 45:23, which states: "To Me every knee shall bend, every tongue swear loyalty." In the verses prior, the prophet called in the name of God upon the "remnants of the nations" (v. 20) to acknowledge that "there is no god beside Me" (v. 21) and he concluded with this passage: "To Me every knee...." The object of loyalty and all authority was the Almighty. In R. Jonathan's epistle, however, the first-person reference was dropped and the entire passage was redirected to Maimonides: "To *him* every knee shall bend, every tongue swear loyalty" (my emphasis).

R. Jonathan modified and combined two complimentary remarks by two famous biblical gentiles to describe the unique vision of Maimonides. The first: when Joseph interpreted Pharaoh's disturbing dreams and offered a plan to thwart the period of famine, Pharaoh announced to all in his court, "Could we find another like him!" (Gen. 41:37). The second: Balaam, the seer from Aram, declared regarding himself that he "beholds visions from the Almighty" (Num. 24:4 and 24:16). R. Jonathan conflated Pharaoh's tribute with Balaam's self-depiction to compliment Maimonides: "Could we find another like him who beholds visions from the Almighty." The words of the Great Master were uniquely and divinely inspired visions, just like those perceived by wise Joseph and the ancient seer, Balaam. Only those were "like him."

R. Jonathan stated that Maimonides "came from Sinai; from Mount Paran he appeared," which he adapted from Deuteronomy 33:2: "The Lord came from Sinai...." R. Jonathan offered the ultimate tribute to Maimonides as one who "revealed" God's Torah to the Jewish nation by means of his *Mishneh Torah*.

In various passages, R. Jonathan complimented Maimonides by attributing to him the roles biblically assigned to the Kohanim (priests). Whereas Malachi (2:7) stated that the "lips of a priest guard knowledge, And men seek rulings from his mouth," R. Jonathan deleted the word "priest" and simply stated regarding Maimonides that "*his* lips guard knowledge" (my emphasis).

Leviticus 10:10 and 10:11 described the roles of the Kohanim in the following language: "(9b) This is a law for all time throughout the ages, (10) for you must distinguish between the sacred and the profane, and between the unclean and the clean; (11) and you must teach the Israelites all the laws which the Lord has imparted to them through Moses." These passages assigned to the priests the task of guarding and interpreting the revealed Law. R. Jonathan modified these verses to declare that God established Maimonides "to be a just teacher.... to teach the Israelites the laws which the Lord had commanded, to distinguish between the unclean and the clean...."

R. Jonathan similarly revised Exodus 19:22—"The priests also, who come near the Lord, must stay pure...."—to the following: "The priests, also, who come near" to him [!] will become purified from the blood of foolishness/error, and "must stay pure." He inverted the subject and object of the verse so that the purity of the priests was dependent upon Maimonides' uncorrupted presence, "lest He break out against them" (v. 24). According to R. Jonathan, Maimonides' role was to protect the Kohanim of his generation—that is, the rabbinic scholars—from imperfection and divine punishment that might occur in response to erroneous teaching or understanding. Given this role, R. Jonathan stated that Maimonides would wear the High Priest's Urim and Thummim (see Ex. 28:30).

Throughout his epistle, R. Jonathan modified biblical verses about the role of Kohanim that he then applied to Maimonides. Since R. Jonathan was a Kohen, this device also entailed a role reversal in which the Lunel Kohen transferred his pedigree to the Egyptian Sage. We noted above (p. 11) that Maimonides (Unit 3) referred to the scholars within R. Jonathan's circle as priests in service of the Lord. Each writer extended priestly status to his correspondent as the ultimate compliment.

R. Jonathan creatively adapted biblical verses and rabbinic interpretations to convey his message. The biblical Moses' name was explicated in Exodus 2:10, in which Pharaoh's daughter "named him 'Moses' ('Moshe'), explaining, 'I drew him out (from "mashah") of the water.'" Although the word "Moshe" was based upon an Egyptian root, *msy*, meaning "to be born," or in its noun form (*ms*), meaning "child"—which means that the princess did not assign him a name but simply called him "child" or "son"—the Bible presented the princess's choice of name as one that was based upon the similar sound of two Hebrew words, Moshe, a proper noun, and the active form of the root, "mashah."[79]

R. Jonathan appropriated this biblical homily and gave it a charming twist to explicate Maimonides' name: "For this [reason] he was named 'Moses,' [for he] rescued [or, 'drew out'] his people from the waters of errors...." In the Bible, ancient Moses was assigned a name that recorded his past and reflected the unique nature of his birth and entrance into the life of his adoptive mother. In R. Jonathan's epistle, the latter-day Moses was assigned a name that foretold his future and his impact on his native kin. R. Jonathan accomplished two objectives with this interpretation. He linked the contemporary Moses with his biblical namesake and, in addition to this compliment by association, paid homage to his MT as a redemptive text for the nation of Israel.

Most of the first half of R. Jonathan's letter entailed homage to Maimonides. Toward the midpoint, he shifted to tribute his *Mishneh Torah*.

His Code was glorified as a source of illumination and blessing and as a unifying factor that made Israel "one nation in the land" (2 Sam., 7:23) or as "one flesh" (Gen. 2:24). In this regard, R. Jonathan acknowledged that the MT had fulfilled one of Maimonides' goals, which he announced in the Introduction to MT, that as a Code it would bring order to the various traditions that grew out of the rich, diverse Talmudic literature.

Two small but unusual points conclude this section of tribute: a prayer that "He [i.e., God, might] give his enemies to drink from the bitter (or poisonous) cup" and an adaptation of Psalm 45:17 (changing the verse from second to third person) that "His sons will succeed his ancestors; he will appoint them princes throughout the land." The curse for Maimonides' enemies seems to be formulaic since, at this point in the history of the *Mishneh Torah* or the "Guide," there were no anti-Maimonidean parties or schools.

The prayer for the ascendancy of his "sons" was surely a standard invocation in accordance with the social norm. Had the Lunel scholars known anything about the family life of Maimonides, they would have referred to his *sole* child—a son, Abraham, who was, at that time, around ten years old[80]—and they would have used language similar to that in the letter from the Geniza, which offered a prayer for "the welfare of his precious one."

These two petitions—for the success of his *Mishneh Torah* and the succession of his seed—were followed by "Amen, amen." Then, a new topic was presented, a request for a copy of Maimonides' *Guide*: "May you, our holy master and teacher, Moses, light of the exile, please give heed to your servants who draw your waters, to satiate us again with the book, '*Guide of the Perplexed*,' regarding which we have heard of its fame, from the land of Egypt, its reputation has gone out."

R. Jonathan remarked that the "Guide's ... reputation has gone out," by which he meant its fame had traversed the Mediterranean and reached the Provencal shores. He complimented Maimonides for this latest scholarly contribution, which warranted international acclaim. The two words that R. Jonathan used—"*yaza tivo*"—"whose fame/reputation has gone out"— also appeared in Maimonides' epistle (Unit 8) in the context of his apology for his tardy response. Whereas R. Jonathan used this phrase to refer to Maimonides' fame for his scholarship as a rabbinic scholar, Maimonides here referred to his reputation as a physician and the overwhelming demands for his medical services. Both authors cited I Samuel 14:47: "And wherever he turned he worsted [them]." R. Jonathan used this passage to depict the convincing and decisive nature of the MT: his Code had overcome all opposition.[81] Right at the start of his *Iggeret*, Maimonides used the same passage to describe the towering scholarly position of R. Jonathan: he overcame all who contested him.

One of the most significant and interesting passages in Maimonides' *Iggeret* (Unit 10) began with his adaptation of Jeremiah 1:5, by which he affirmed his lifelong engagement with Torah study.

> And I, Moses, declare to the revered Rabbi, R. Jonathan the Cohen—and to all the scholars and their colleagues who will read my letter—that 'before I was created in the womb the Torah selected me; and before I was born, it consecrated me to its study' (see Jer. 1:5). I was designated 'to cause her springs to gush forth' (see Pr. 5:16). She is my 'loving doe' (see Pr. 5:19), the 'wife of my youth' (see Pr. 5:18); 'my love of her has been my infatuation since my youth' (see Pr. 5:19).

The Jeremiah adaptation was crucial to his final apology, which followed in the next lines. In this sequence—which I shall analyze later in detail—he referred to his seduction to other forms of *hokhmah*, which he compared to Solomon's "foreign wives." Prior to that admission, he needed to affirm his essential engagement with Torah study; he chose the Jeremiah image to do so.

Maimonides' objective in this unit was to offer another apology for his tardy response and to establish a positive and collegial relationship with the Lunel scholars. In this sequence, he shared with these scholars his ideological position on worldly knowledge, its relationship to Jewish learning, and the legitimate claim it had upon him. These elegantly crafted passages are some of the most memorable in the entire *Iggeret*.

His choice of the Jeremiah passage warrants examination since it seems a bit self-aggrandizing. With these verses, he announced how the "Torah selected me … before I was born" and how "it consecrated me to its study." If his objective was to confirm his genuine engagement with Jewish scholarship, he could have accomplished that satisfactorily by the various Proverbs passages. In those verses, he rehearsed his infatuation with his "loving doe," the "wife of my youth" with whom he has been infatuated since his youth. Those lines affirmed his love affair with Torah scholarship and his choice to "cause her springs to gush…." In the context of his attempt to reach out to these men as colleagues and equals, the boastful language of Jeremiah regarding his interuterine selection set him apart from the Lunel scholars.

When we read R. Jonathan's epistles, however, we discover that it was R. Jonathan who first used the Jeremiah verses. In the first letter, he adapted in rhyme the verb roots and terminologies of Jeremiah 1:5 to declare that Maimonides, like the prophet Jeremiah, had been selected by God while still within his mother's womb.[82] In his second letter, R. Jonathan returned to the same passage as a finale of the poem he had placed at the start of that text.

> Hearken, the plaint of the daughter Jerusalem:
> All glory has fallen into the lot of Egypt.
> There Divine Presence has a holy encampment and there
> Is the altar of the Lord, a delight to the eyes:
> His chosen one, Moses, who alone remains
> Worthy to be a prophet among all the sons of Ephraim.
> Before He formed him, He knew him, hallowed him, for His sacred law,
> That thirsty ones may find in him water to drink.[83]

R. Jonathan apparently considered this passage to be a particularly appropriate tribute to Maimonides. By these creative adaptations, he praised him as a historic teacher of Israel who had been selected by God in the same fashion as He had designated prophets in biblical times.

When Maimonides' epistle is read contextually as a response to R. Jonathan, his choice of terminology is understood differently. Maimonides was not the one who fashioned a boastful comparison to the great prophet Jeremiah. He merely repeated in his *Iggeret* an image that R. Jonathan had used to compliment, in dramatic and biblical terminology, Maimonides' lifelong association with Torah and Jewish thought.

Maimonides also incorporated a complex Midrashic interpretation that R. Jonathan cited.[84] Talmud, Sotah 37b calculated that the Israelites entered into multiple covenants with God—as many as forty-eight!—for each commandment in the Torah. Also, the Israelites served as "guarantors for guarantors" to doubly enforce the communal pledge of acceptance of the Torah. R. Jonathan referred explicitly to this midrash regarding the forty-eight "britot (covenants)" and later applied the Aramaic phrase contained in that Talmudic discussion to Maimonides, saying that he served as "guarantor for the guarantors." The reference to the multiple covenants was clearly drawn from this passage in the Talmud.

In his *Iggeret*, Maimonides wrote regarding the school of R. Jonathan that

> It was long ago decreed that it is yours to interpret and teach the statutes and the laws; for you are the guardians (see Deut. 33:9) of "the words of the Lord [which] are pure words" (Ps. 12:7)—guardians of the Covenants (see Deut. 33:9 and Sotah 37b) as in former years.

In this tribute to the Lunel scholars, applying a priestly role to them as teachers and interpreters, the term "guardians of the Covenant" may have been taken from Deuteronomy 33:9, which entailed Moses' testament to the tribes of Israel. Deuteronomy 33:9 is part of the tribute to Levi, who will have the responsibility to wear the Thummim and Urim (v. 8), and to teach God's "laws to Jacob." Deuteronomy 33:9 stated: "Your precepts alone they observed, And kept Your covenant." The tribe of Levi, from whom the Kohanim were derived, would be diligent in guarding the Covenant between Israel and the Lord. Maimonides complimented R. Jonathan and the other Kohanim with him who sustained that Levitical role.

In describing the Covenant that the Lunel circle preserved, however, Maimonides referred it in the plural—"guardians of the covenants"—"britot." The plural makes no sense unless Maimonides was constructing these lines upon the midrash of Sotah 37b, which R. Jonathan had cited. In his *Iggeret*, Maimonides unquestionably drew upon the terminology and imagery of the midrash that R. Jonathan had incorporated in his text.

My comparison of R. Jonathan's composition with Maimonides' *Iggeret* demonstrates that they contain numerous shared elements. These can be grouped in two categories:

1. <u>Similarity of language</u> (i.e., shared words or images):
   a. I Samuel 14:47—"he worsted them"
   b. "*yaza tivo*"—"his fame had gone out"
   c. Jeremiah 1:5—interuterine designation of Jeremiah/ Maimonides
   d. Sotah 37b—multiple Covenants

2. <u>Similarity of rhetoric</u> (i.e., shared motives, structure, or content/themes):
   a. dramatic opening passage regarding sending/reception of the epistle

b. identification of the cultural, east/west locus of the correspondents
c. projection of priestly status upon the correspondent
d. application of modified biblical passages regarding God, Moses, or other biblical figures to Maimonides

When these letters are read sequentially, many elements within Maimonides' epistle read as a direct response to R. Jonathan's epistles. We might conclude, upon examining the letter to R. Anatoli and the two received from R. Jonathan, that we have unraveled the creative process Maimonides followed in the development of his Lunel responsum. One can imagine Maimonides preparing his epistle to R. Jonathan, holding his earlier letter to R. Anatoli in one hand and R. Jonathan's epistles in the other.

There is another interpretation, however, which accounts for the many common elements shared by these letters. Possibly these various epistles contained standard elements of the epistolary genre; maybe each was a (creative?) turn on the models that were extant at that time?

Many questions follow that assumption, the following of which are germane to this study. Do we find many letters from the Late Middle Ages in which correspondents quoted and/or reversed the formulations of their interlocutors? Possibly this kind of rhetoric was perceived as a tribute to the original author, whose words warranted repetition, expansion, or commentary by the respondent?

I charted above fifty-five biblical passages that Maimonides incorporated within his *Iggeret*. Was his choice of biblical texts distinctive, reflecting his own mastery of the Hebrew Bible, the ideas he formulated in this correspondence, and his creative response to R. Jonathan's letter? Or might we find many of these verses in other epistles composed during that epoch? Perhaps these passages were the "favorites" that many authors incorporated in their writings?

Was the proportion of biblical passages found, in one fashion or another, in Maimonides' letter typical of other epistles of that epoch? And how did adaptations of biblical passages appear in different periods and cultural groups? Can we identify styles of adaptation that differed by author, culture, period, and so forth?

Within my analysis of the *Iggeret*, I reflected that some biblical adaptations seemed irreverent, as when passages about God, a prophet, or even the Kohanim were redirected to (mortal) Maimonides. Was there an ethic of adaptation that set the standard? Was this practice widespread within all cultural/ethnic groups? Was there a norm or acceptable range for these adaptations?[85]

One example from my discussion above will illustrate the significance of this distinction. I proposed above that R. Jonathan's letter was the source for the Jeremiah image that Maimonides included in his letter. It seemed clear to me that Maimonides borrowed it from his correspondent's text. However, the Jeremiah passage may have been a trope used by many authors to compliment (possibly in panegyric fashion) their correspondent? When Maimonides incorporated the Jeremiah image in his letter, he might have done so because it was a popular and frequently used image in epistolary correspondence at that time. His source might have been the contemporary literary milieu rather than R. Jonathan's letter.

The answer to questions such as these would allow us to appreciate these epistles as they were perceived by the generations that composed/read them.

B. Z. Baneth, in his *Iggrot ha-Rambam* (*Letters of the Rambam*), offered a brief discussion of the structure of epistolary style.[86] He observed that one letter written by Maimonides was written in the style of rhymed prose letters of the period … and, like many such letters, one may divide the letter in to four sections:

1. praise of the letter's recipient,
2. acknowledgment of receipt of the letter (which had been previously sent by the recipient of this letter) and praises regarding it,
3. the main body (content) of the letter,
4. [closing] salutations.

Baneth did not accompany his remarks with citations of other letters to illustrate and document epistolary style.

When I applied Baneth's four-part structure to the epistle to R. Jonathan, I noted that Maimonides' letter contained six units, as follows:

a. Praises of R. Jonathan and the scholars as guardians and teachers of Torah; prayer for R. Jonathan's well-being (Units 1–3);

    b. Tribute to their letters (i.e., their epistle plus the twenty-four questions; Units 4 and 5);
    c. Reflection on rhymed prose and announcement regarding reversal to unadorned prose (transitional Unit 6);
    d. Main body:
        i. reiteration (in unadorned prose) of Maimonides' joy at R. Jonathan's questions (i.e., his scholarship);
        ii. Maimonides' declaration of the historic role of Provencal scholars (Unit 7);
        iii. Extended apology for tardy response—five justifications (Units 8–10);
    e. Tribute to codification of Jewish law in the MT and invitation for corrections (Unit 11);
    f. Salutation and final blessing (Unit 12).

    Baneth's four-part structure can be identified in many of the other epistles examined here. However, to a certain extent, these elements and their sequence are found in most letters. If one is composing a letter in response to a correspondent, one usually begins by acknowledging or referring to the correspondent's initial letter, thanking the correspondent for it. In the event that one's response had been delayed, an apology will usually follow the acknowledgment of receipt. The next unit would be the core of the letter, presenting the essential theme(s) or purposes of the correspondence. (In Maimonides' letters, the apology for tardiness was often the principal objective of the letter.) After the main content of the letter, one usually concludes with a salutation, often including wishes for the well-being of the recipient. Thus, the structure that Baneth identified as the norm for rhymed prose epistles of the Middle Ages is one that guides most social compositions to this day.

    A study of epistolary style would enable modern readers to understand Maimonides in the context of his milieu, and would have enabled us to appreciate whether his *Iggeret* was typical of the genre or an exceptional composition. Unfortunately, a full scholarly examination of epistolary style has not been done.[87] Decter comments: "There has not yet been a comprehensive treatment of Jewish letter writing based on Geniza materials and in light of Arabic epistolary practices that takes into account the full range of stylistic differences across period, location and social rank, though there have been various localized treatments."[88]

Assuredly, the inclusion of R. Jonathan's epistle together with the Lunel questions dramatically altered the nature of this correspondence. If the Lunel scholars had presented only their twenty-four questions to Maimonides, he would have authored responsa to these questions as he did in all such exchanges, focusing exclusively on their subject matter. Since R. Jonathan elected to accompany the twenty-four with a rhymed prose epistle, a new element was added that motivated Maimonides to respond in kind. The result was a gift that warranted not only this study but our unending admiration for the depth and range of the teachings and writings of the Grand Rabbi, Moshe ben Maimon.

Chapter 6

The Second Half of the *Iggeret* in Unadorned Prose

Most of the second half of the epistle entailed Maimonides' apology to the Lunel community for his delayed response to their inquiry. Maimonides apparently was so eager to justify his delay that, after his announcement about his style reversal (in Unit 6), he presented a total of five different explanations (in Units 8, 9, and 10). Before this apology, he repeated (in Unit 7) some of the themes he had treated earlier in the rhymed prose half of the epistle. But in this part—which has been divided below into three sentences for ease of analysis—Maimonides addressed his correspondents in language that was elegant but direct, clear, and without poetic flourishes.

1. I, Moses, declare to you—R. Jonathan, Rabbi and Kohen—that when your letter and your questions reached me, I was truly overjoyed on account of them.
2. I said to myself, "Blessed be the Lord, who has not withheld a redeemer from you ...." (Ruth 4:14). For I understood that my words had reached someone who understood their content, who comprehended their inner meanings, and who could debate and discuss them appropriately. I said to myself, he "will renew your life and sustain your old age" (Ruth 4:15).
3. All [the questions] you asked, you asked well; all the difficult questions you posed, you posed well. "Fear not, for I am with you" (Is. 43:5).

By comparing this unit with the opening in the rhymed prose section we readily perceive how Maimonides has departed from the road of Sephardic-style rhetoric. The first part of the *Iggeret* was a dramatic poetic construction that, to use Prof. Twersky's words (see p. 16), was composed "solely for rhetorical effect." In Unit 7, Maimonides returned to the topic of his reception of the Lunel letters, but this time with language that was simple and clear. Maimonides assured R. Jonathan that he welcomed the Lunel critique of his MT, and took particular pleasure at the quality of their twenty-four questions. He delighted that his "words had reached someone who understood their content, who comprehended their inner meanings, and who could debate and discuss them appropriately."[89]

As in the rhymed prose section of the letter, he included here a series of praises about his correspondents. But whereas in the rhymed prose section Maimonides lauded them as majestic warriors in battle on behalf of the Torah, Kohanim and guardians of the Law, here he tributed their role in terms of their relationship to him. He portrayed these unknown scholars as vital colleagues—redeemers—who would play a historic role in sustaining his legacy. I shall discuss this more extensively below.

Maimonides again used conversion as a literary device to portray his relationship to the Lunel scholars. In the rhymed prose section, the Provencal letters were initially perceived as an affirming correspondence that, upon examination, became a challenging threat. In the unadorned part, the conversion moved in the opposite direction: the letters initially perceived as challenges were subsequently depicted as redeeming texts that would sustain Maimonides' MT and preserve his legacy.

Now that Maimonides had depicted his positive attitude toward the Provencal scholars and their correspondence, he had to justify his delay in responding to them. He presented three causes in Unit 8: his illnesses, "a multitude of disturbances," and his demanding medical practice. In various writings from different periods, Maimonides referred to bouts of illness, both physical and emotional. For example, he wrote movingly to R. Japheth, a judge in Acre, that for a year he was in a deep depression after his brother drowned (c. 1177).[90] He wrote to R. Phinehas, the Provencal scholar who became the judge in Alexandria in the early 1190s, that he was "ill, near death." It is not known whether Maimonides' remarks to R. Phinehas accurately recorded a life-threatening illness.[91] Possibly, Maimonides inflated his sickness in the context of apologies to his correspondents.[92]

Next, he referred to a "multitude of disturbances" that delayed him. He did not provide any specifics. Given that he will refer to his overwhelming medical practice in the next sentence, he could not be referring to it here in this remark. The reference remains ambiguous.

Maimonides referred to his exhausting medical practice in many of his writings. Most well-known is his letter to Samuel Ibn Tibbon,[93] who had been asked by R. Jonathan to translate Maimonides' *Guide*. Ibn Tibbon requested an audience with Maimonides to benefit from the author's critique of his translation; Maimonides replied that he did not have time for a meeting. He wrote Ibn Tibbon a lengthy explanation of his refusal, with his now well-known and heart-wrenching portrait of his overwhelming daily schedule as a physician, compounded by his communal and rabbinic responsibilities. This letter to Ibn Tibbon, which probably was composed after the *Iggeret* to R. Jonathan, was the last exchange between the Sage of Fustat and French Jewry.

> I dwell at Fustat, and the sultan resides at Cairo [about a mile and a half away].... My duties to the sultan are very heavy. I am obliged to visit him every day, early in the morning; and when he or any of his children, or any of the inmates of his harem, are indisposed. I dare not quit Cairo, but must stay during the greater part of the day in the palace. It also frequently happens that one or two of the two royal officers fall sick, and I must attend to their healing. Hence, as a rule, I repair to Cairo very early in the day, and if nothing unusual happens, I do not return to Fustat until the afternoon. Then I am almost dying with hunger. I find the antechamber filled with people, both Jews and Gentiles, nobles and common people, judges and bailiffs, friends and foes—a mixed multitude, who await the time of my return.
>
> I dismount from my animal, wash my hands, go forth to my patients, and entreat them to bear with me while I partake of some slight refreshment, the only meal I take in the twenty-four hours. Then I attend to my patients, write prescriptions for their various ailments. Patients go in and out until nightfall, and sometimes even, I solemnly assure you, until two hours and more in the night. I converse with and prescribe for them while lying down from sheer fatigue, and when night falls, I am so exhausted that I can scarcely speak.
>
> In consequence of this, no Israelite can have any private interview with me except on the Sabbath. On this day the whole congregation, or at least the majority of the members, come to me after the morning service, when I instruct them as to their proceedings during the whole week; we study together a little until noon, when they depart. Some of them return, and read with me after the afternoon service until evening prayers. In this manner I spend that day.[94]

In addition to his medical practice, Maimonides was extensively engaged in the composition of medical works, whether in the context of his own medical research or on behalf of various patrons. Herbert Davidson, in his biography *Maimonides: The Man and His Works*, wrote the following regarding Maimonides' medical training, practice, and medical compositions:

> The event that impelled Maimonides into the full-time practice of medicine was undoubtedly the death by drowning of his young brother in approximately 1177. The tragedy left Maimonides with debts and the responsibility for the family's livelihood.... But the obvious way out of his financial straits was the practice of medicine, a subject that he had studied in his youth, before arriving in Egypt.... by the early 1190s, he had become a well-known physician with a clientele in the highest echelons....
>
> The sole substantial writings known to have come out of the years from 1191 to the end of his life are medical works. Preparing books on medicine for both laymen and physicians swallowed up whatever productive time remained after he had treated his patients and pored over the medical literature pertinent to their cases.[95]

Davidson listed ten medical texts that were written by Maimonides in addition to three others whose authenticity is uncertain.

From Maimonides' description of his medical responsibilities to Samuel Ibn Tibbon and the various medical treatises that have survived, we readily appreciate the excessive demands upon him as physician/medical scholar during the period when he received the Lunel letters.

It was unlikely that these men, prior to this correspondence, were aware of Maimonides' expertise and fame in a field other than Torah. In his letter, R. Jonathan noted how Maimonides' reputation "had gone out" because of the many books he had written in different domains of Judaic scholarship.

As I noted above, Maimonides refers to his fame in the context of reviewing his medical activities: "The yoke of responsibility for the health care of the gentiles which is upon my shoulders has dissipated my strength. They do not leave me one free hour, day or night. But what can I do, now that I have acquired fame in so many lands?" (*Iggeret* Unit 8). In essence, he declares that his fame as a physician overcame his reputation as a Judaic scholar. This tension will surface in a different guise in another passage to be discussed below.

In Unit 9, he offered another justification for his delay.

> In addition, I am today not like I was in my youth. My strength has become weak, I am dejected, impatient, my speech is slow, my hands tremble—I tarry even when it comes to writing a brief letter. For this reason, please do not be offended that I arranged for someone else to transcribe my responses [i.e., to the twenty-four questions] and some of my letters [to you]. I did not write everything in my own hand because I didn't have free time for such things because of my weakened physical condition and impatient spirit, and because of those who pester me at all times.

With remarkable—and surprising—candor, he shared with these men some personal information about his aging and emotional state, both of which impeded his rejoinder. He referred not only to the physical effects of age, but to his psychological well-being, which was also challenged by the combination of advanced age and the unrelenting pressures of his medical and communal responsibilities.

If Maimonides wished to assure the Lunel group that he meant no discourtesy to them by his delayed response, and that he had the highest regard for their scholarship and questions, these four justifications should have been sufficient. Yet, in this epistle, he added another justification that differed radically from the others.

> And I, Moses, declare to the revered Rabbi, R. Jonathan the Kohen—and to all the scholars and their colleagues who will read my letter—that 'before I was created in the womb the Torah selected me; and before I was born, it consecrated me to its study' (see Jer. 1:5). I was designated 'to cause her springs to gush forth' (see Pr. 5:16). She is my 'loving doe' (see Pr. 5:19), the 'wife of my youth' (see Pr. 5:18); 'my love of her has been my infatuation since my youth' (see Pr. 5:19).
>
> Nonetheless, [others: "many"] "foreign women" became her rival-wives—"Moabite, Ammonite, Edomite, Phoenician, and Hittite women" (see I Kings 11:1). God knows that, initially, they were only taken to be her [assistants as] "perfumers, chefs, bakers" (I Sam. 8:13)—"to display her beauty to the peoples and the officials; for she was a[96] beautiful woman" (Est. 1:11). However, her time for sexual congress became diminished (based upon Ex. 21:10) because my heart was divided into many parts by so many fields of knowledge.

The first four causes for Maimonides' delayed response were factors he could not control. He could not deter his aging or his illness, nor could he effectively refuse to treat his commanding patron, the Vizier, other powerful individuals demanding medical treatises, or his numerous patients. This fifth and final justification differed from the others in that it was the result of his ideological position and the choices he made in the allocation of his scholarly undertakings. With remarkable candor—and wonderful style—Maimonides revealed that another competing demand upon his time delayed his response: his engagement in the study of *hokhmah*, other "fields of knowledge."

The term *hokhmah* was used by Maimonides and medieval scholars to refer to the study of philosophy, the sciences—as perceived during that time period—or human knowledge, in a general sense. Maimonides reported that these studies were initially undertaken to advance the appreciation of Torah, just as good assistant cooks (i.e., "perfumers, chefs, bakers") prepare side dishes that accompany and enhance the main course of a banquet.[97] However, with the passing of time, these "foreign women" became co-wives and competitors for his affection. Ultimately, his time for conjugal bliss with the love of his life—the study of Torah—had to compete with these branches of wisdom.

Maimonides did not repudiate or apologize for his engagement with *hokhmah*. His attitude toward the interconnectedness of Torah and other fields of knowledge was explicit and paramount. His engagement with *hokhmah* was an essential element of his personal and scholarly life.[98] In this epistle, Maimonides shared with these men his inner torment as he struggled to balance his ideological and scholarly passions, devoting sufficient time to Torah but also to *hokhmah*. His vivid description of a heart "divided into many parts by so many fields of knowledge" resonates loudly today to anyone so afflicted.

This conflict was an issue that was vital to Maimonides' ideology. He referenced it in his very first work—the *Commentary to the Mishnah*—finished when he was thirty years old, ten years before his MT and many decades before the *Iggeret*. In the concluding words of his *Commentary*, Maimonides requested readers to advise him of any errors in his composition. He shared with his readers that he composed the *Commentary* during a politically unstable period, and often did his writing while on ship as he traversed the Mediterranean. Given the tumultuous context, he feared that he might have erred in his text. He also noted that another possible cause for errors might be his "being engaged in other sciences."

At this early age, Maimonides deemed it necessary to acknowledge that his expansive appreciation of diverse fields of wisdom—"other sciences"—could result in errors in his writings about Torah. In this remarkable section of his *Iggeret*, the Grand Rabbi reiterated this theme. He bared his heart to these men by declaring that his delayed response to their correspondence was because he was too busy studying Aristotle.

If we examine the biblical passage he cited, however, his message was actually more complex and even daring. The words he used—"foreign women" and their ethnic or political backgrounds (i.e., "Moabite, Ammonite," etc.)—were taken from I Kings 11:1, which Maimonides knew would be recognized by these scholars. He probably assumed they would have noticed that he cited those terms out of context, thereby avoiding the warning it conveyed. The full sequence reads as follows:

> King Solomon loved many foreign women ... Moabite, Ammonite, Edomite, Phoenician, Hittite women, from the nations of which the Lord had said ... none of them shall join you, lest they turn your heart away to follow their gods. ... In his old age, his wives turned away Solomon's heart after other gods, and he was not as wholeheartedly devoted to the Lord his God as his father David had been. (I Kings 11: 1–3)

These verses were a protest against alliances with "foreign women." Despite Solomon's kingly objective to establish politically beneficial relationships with his wives' nations of origin, his fascination with and passion for "The Other" brought about a lessening of devotion to the God of Israel. With astounding candor, Maimonides compared his dalliance in other fields of wisdom with Solomon's marital alliances, which ultimately corrupted his reign. By invoking this passage, even in part, Maimonides revealed his awareness that his passion for other fields of knowledge could impact, in various ways, his love affair with the Torah of Israel. In this instance, he admitted that it—minimally—caused a delay in his response to the Provencal questions.

By drawing upon this biblical passage, he acknowledged the potential harm that could result from an embrace of other fields of study and knowledge. By introducing I Kings 11:1, Maimonides shared with these men his inner ideological torment as he strove to balance his lifelong passion for Torah study with competing scholarly interests in other fields of knowledge. He complimented these Lunel scholars by his honest declaration of his ideology, probably founded on his vision of these men as individuals who might have appreciated his engagement in many fields of knowledge. The Provencal community had contacted him regarding astrology, and they had requested a copy of his *Guide*. They could understand the cost his all-encompassing study had on his heart and mind as well as upon his time.

Maimonides' engagement with *hokhmah* impacted one of his responsa to the Lunel scholars. Responsum 315 can be interpreted as a unique instance in which Maimonides utilized his knowledge of science or worldly knowledge in a halakhic context.[99] The Lunel rabbis questioned his position (Laws of Slaughter 8:16 and 8:23; 10:9 [subsection 52]) that a missing upper mandible of an animal rendered it *treif* (not kosher). They pointed out that whereas the Mishnah stated that an animal with a missing lower mandible is not *treif*, the texts were silent regarding an upper jaw. "We, in our humble opinion, have never heard of this [decision] until now, nor have we seen this [law] written in any code in any language…."

Maimonides first confirmed that the Talmudic discussion was only about the lower jaw; then, he continued with a mini-course in bovine anatomy. Given these anatomical facts, "there is no better example of a defect with which an animal could not survive than this [i.e., a missing upper mandible]." He concluded: "Regarding what you stated, that you have never learned or read in any code an opinion which counted this as 'treif'—there are many things that the commentaries do not mention because they did not put their minds to such issues. If they understood such things, they would see [i.e., agree with me]."

Maimonides defended his position in the MT on the basis of his knowledge of *hokhmah*, which he was willing to apply to determine Jewish law although his position lacked Talmudic or rabbinic precedent.[100]

A later authority, R. Isaac bar Sheshet (known by his acronym, "Rivash"; 1326–1408) disagreed forcefully with Maimonides on this point:

> … you understand that we do not determine laws of our Torah and its commandments according to the scholars of science and medicine, for if we would affirm [our laws] in accordance with their opinions, the Torah would not be "from Heaven," heaven forbid.… If we would determine matters regarding "treifot" in accordance with medical scholars, we would receive much reward from the butchers [since some "treif" animals would be healed or otherwise considered viable and kosher].… Moreover, when Maimonides, of blessed memory, offered a different ruling [Laws of Slaughter 8:14, regarding a law of "treifot"] they [i.e., the Rabad, ad loc.]

> did not agree with him.... Even though the Rabbi, of blessed memory, was a scholar of medicine, science and an expert in surgery, we do not base our law upon [the knowledge of] science and medicine.... We do not believe in the Greek or Arab scholars who established their positions on the basis of speculation ["s'vara"] and upon some [prior] experience, without being [sufficiently] attentive to various doubts/problems that occur with that [prior] experience.[101]

Rivash held Maimonides in highest esteem. In another responsum, he partnered him with R. Alfasi as worthy of utmost consideration by all rabbinic scholars since they were "authorities acclaimed by the [entire] Jewish world and they are pillars of the Torah."[102] Although he harbored reservations about following the MT blindly without prior mastery of the relevant Talmudic and rabbinic sources,[103] Rivash cited Maimonides most frequently of all the authorities of the Spanish school.[104] Nonetheless, he could not countenance Maimonides' distinctive integration of *hokhmah* within the realm of rabbinic jurisprudence.[105]

Thus, in Unit 10, Maimonides presented to the Lunel scholars a justification for his delayed response that reflected his ideology. Although the study of what others considered "foreign" material could weaken one's faith or, in a less substantial fashion, detract from time devoted to Torah study and teaching, Maimonides was committed to full engagement with valuable wisdom in all disciplines, regardless of origin.

Having justified his delayed response, Maimonides then proceeded in the next unit of the *Iggeret* to address the Lunel scholars directly and personally, sharing with them his deeply held objectives that drove him to compose the MT. He stated:

> How I labored—day and night—for some ten consecutive years, putting together this composition. Great men like you will understand what I have done since I brought together things that were scattered and dispersed (see Esther 3:8) between hills and mountains.

The tone and the substance of this segment suggest that Maimonides saw these men as his colleagues—"great men" with whom he could converse in confidence. He had studied their twenty-four questions and from them he had gained a sense of their scholarship. Since they were masters of the Talmudic texts, they would be able to ascertain the sources upon which he had based his decisions. They would not focus on the lack of textual proof within the Code, as other scholars did, but would have the knowledge and depth to deal with his work in an appropriate scholarly fashion.

Before such scholars, Maimonides could speak openly about his MT with pride; they appreciated its uniqueness and would not consider his remark boastful or conceited. He shared with them his main objectives in composing the MT.

> My intent in this treatise was to clear up the roads and to remove the stumbling blocks from before the students so their minds would not grow weary from the many complicated exchanges [in the Talmud and classic rabbinic texts] which might end in an error in legal decision-making.

When he identified its singular accomplishment, he highlighted the MT's role as an accessible compendium of the diverse and complex legal material within the Talmudic literature. It would serve as a source for accurate halakhic decision-making since most students were unable to negotiate the tortuous dialectic of Talmudic texts and reasoning, and therefore were unable to render proper decisions.

Maimonides then invited his colleagues to critique and correct his Code.

> But, "who can be aware of errors?" (Ps. 19:13) and forgetfulness is a common occurrence for everybody, but even more for the elderly. So for all these reasons it is appropriate to search through my words and to check up after me. A reader of my treatise should not say, "For what will the man be like who will succeed the one who is ruling?" (Eccl. 2:12). Rather, I hereby grant him permission: "'Let him enter,' said the king" (Est. 6:5). You scholars have done me a great favor, and so has anyone else who finds something [in error] and informs me. He has done me a favor so that there will not remain [in the book] any misleading error, Heaven forbid.

Maimonides' expression of appreciation for the "great favor" that these scholars had already accomplished and his invitation for correction were genuine. His invitation related to two classes of errors: (1) legal decisions within the MT that were incorrect; (2) textual errors in the MT text due to a copyist's error or other material causes. In their twenty-four questions, these scholars had already demonstrated their ability to present both kinds of criticisms.

In response to one question (regarding his decision in Laws of Fringes, 2:7)[106] Maimonides commented succinctly:

> In truth, this [law] is certainly in accordance with your position. In accordance with those principles I have corrected my text since I erred.... And thus you also should correct your text [Maimonides here provides the corrected text].

The most important word in his responsum was "emet"—truth. Maimonides immediately recognized that "I erred." He corrected his text and, for formality's sake, reviewed in his letter what the new, authoritative—and truthful—text should be.

One of the standard commentators on the MT, R. Shem Tov Ibn Gaon (late thirteenth—early fourteenth century), in his commentary *Migdal Oz* (ad loc.), stated:

> "Study his ways and learn" (Prov. 6:6)—he did not use the pretext of claiming that this was a scribe's error. Instead, he admitted that "I erred"....

This was, however, the only instance within the twenty-four questions in which Maimonides acceded to the Lunel criticism. In every other case, he either rebutted their argument or identified their question as the result of a flawed MT manuscript.

He began Responsum 326[107] by complimenting his correspondents: "This question is surely one that a scholar would ask. For a long while, I thought about this matter...." After presenting the sources that brought him to his conclusion, he ended with the following: "This is how it seemed to me, and may the Lord save me from error." Maimonides defended and maintained the position he had codified in his MT. Yet, since he considered the Lunel question to be a strong one—as he himself pondered when he wrote his Code—he was moved to end his responsum with a prayer that his decision, indeed, was free from error.

In another responsum[108] Maimonides repeated his high regard for the rabbis and called them "his colleagues," after which he proceeded to chide them for their question.

> Do not belittle yourselves. If you are not to be considered as my Masters, you are my colleagues, my companions, my friends. All that you questioned is worthy of being questioned. The Heads of the Academies in Babylonia also criticized this section when the Compilation reached them (and they also

questioned some minor matters that you—Heaven forbid—would not have questioned). Nonetheless, all of your questions did not penetrate the matter deeply enough.

After first complimenting the Lunel scholars, he gently criticized their question as superficial. Within those remarks he threw in a bit of rabbinic gossip that reflected his tense relationship with some members of the Babylonian scholarly community. Maimonides had engaged in some public debates with the Heads of the Academies in Baghdad over his MT and other writings.[109] In the context of acknowledging the insight of the French scholars, Maimonides made an oblique remark that displayed his low regard and inner resentment for his critics in the East. Although he reported that the Heads of the Babylonian academies questioned his MT with the same objection presented by the Lunel rabbis (in Question 300), the Babylonian rabbis also asked questions that you—"heaven forbid"— would never have asked. One can only wonder how this aside was received by the French scholars who, unlike us, did not have access to the exchanges between Baghdad and the Sage of Fustat.

Maimonides concluded this responsum with a six-line demonstration to sustain his decision in the MT. He rebutted the Lunel—and Babylonian—critiques. But then he tacked on a finale to the responsum that was his honest acknowledgment that the question raised by scholars East and West was a reasonable one: "This is my opinion in this matter, but one who wishes to disagree on this may do so."

Maimonides had good reason to invite these men to continue their review of the text of his MT. When Maimonides studied the Lunel questions, he found that not less than four of the set were based upon an incorrect MT text.[110] For example, when the French scholars expressed surprise at one of his decisions in the MT, Maimonides responded:

That which you stated....I too had not heard until today. Inform me where in my writings this error is found....This is the [correct] text and if the text that has reached you contains something that contradicts this, as you have written, it is assuredly a scribe's error. Correct my text! (Responsum 316)[111]

And again:

You have no criticism against me... nor against yourselves. Rather, [it should be directed to] the scribe or the one who copied [over his text]. This is the [correct] version of my words: …. The words that you quoted … are a total error from the scribe or from the copier. Correct the book! (Responsum 354)[112]

Another responsum records a different cause for textual inaccuracy. Maimonides wrote:

This too is a mistake [i.e., flawed text], but the criticism is not [to be directed] to the copier but because the first edition of the book went out [i.e., was copied] from the galleys [which contained these words] not in the correct place. I have by now already added something which was not in that first version, which is.... You too should add those words so that the reading of the text will be thus....

The wellsprings of wisdom were stopped up not on your account, but because of the pen. The pen stopped them up; it will now uncover the depths of wisdom. (Responsum 433)[113]

In this responsum, Maimonides acknowledged that in his first draft of this section of the MT he rendered a decision that he subsequently changed for the very reasons mentioned by the Lunel rabbis. Although he had discovered and corrected his error in his final edition, there were some who were so eager to obtain the teaching of the Great Master that they copied and distributed an MT codex prematurely, prior to his final review and approval. The MT text that the Lunel scholars had received, apparently, was based upon this earlier edition.

From Maimonides' response to the set of Lunel questions, we may conclude that he was confident that future correspondence with these scholars would be productive.[114] They had already proved their mettle; Maimonides' commitment to objective scholarship surely informed his invitation to them to sustain their criticism of his works—in both regards. His request that the conversation continue was surely genuine.

The final unit of his *Iggeret* was a prayer: "May the Omnipresent, Blessed Be He, assist us and you in [our] study of His Law and in our understanding of His Unity, and may we not stumble." Maimonides extended his demonstration of collegiality to the end of his epistle, petitioning that God "assist us and you in [our] study of his Law...." Maimonides viewed his correspondents as members of a fellowship of Torah scholars. He addressed them here as his own students: May "the Omnipresent ... assist us and You ... in our understanding"—he prayed for all of them, together.[115]

Chapter 7

Maimonides and the Lunel Scholars—Reconsidered

The unadorned prose section of Maimonides' *Iggeret* was an unexpectedly personal communication. Although Maimonides complimented R. Jonathan for the quality of his questions and assured him that they were a welcomed communication, he did not treat the content or character of the Lunel correspondence nor did he develop a poetic tribute to Torah scholarship.

In this half of his epistle, Maimonides focused upon his relationship to the Lunel scholars: he devoted most of this section to his apology for his tardy response, providing a variety of justifications for the delay. What prompted this elaborate apology? Why didn't he simply send R. Jonathan a review of his daily schedule as he later sent Ibn Tibbon, and that should have been sufficient?

In the context of these justifications, Maimonides revealed much about himself, his physical and emotional health, overwhelming medical practice, the goals and objectives that drove him to compose his grand *Hibbur*, and his understanding of the relationship and role of Torah and *hokhmah*. His epistle to these strangers from Provence provided them—and us—with a window on his soul.

There are other epistles in which Maimonides was quite self-revelatory—such as his letter to Samuel Ibn Tibbon—and some contained material or themes that he treated in the *Iggeret* to R. Jonathan. In those cases, however, Maimonides had a relationship with the recipient that justified the personal nature of his writing or there were other obvious reasons for expressing himself in such a fashion.[116] The richness of his response—its length and personally revealing nature—suggested that there may have been other factors that moved Maimonides to address this group of scholars so intimately.

In addition, there remains the question regarding the style reversal of the unadorned prose section of the *Iggeret*: what was so vital in this half of the epistle that Maimonides found it necessary to abandon rhymed prose "so this matter can be appropriately considered?"

In the second part of the epistle, Maimonides used two phrases to highlight ideas that were significant to him and pivotal in this epistle: "I, Moses, declare" and "I said to myself." Maimonides used the phrase "I, Moses, declare" in Units 7 and 10. The first occurrence was at the opening of the unadorned prose section of the epistle (Unit 7), immediately following his disparaging statement about rhymed prose and the announcement of his style reversal.

> I, Moses, declare to you—R. Jonathan, Rabbi and Kohen—that when your letter and your questions reached me, I was truly overjoyed on account of them. I said to myself, "Blessed be the Lord, who has not withheld a redeemer from you…. (Ruth 4:14).

Maimonides could have simply stated, "When your correspondence and your questions arrived, I was truly overjoyed on account of them." His opening—"I, Moses, declare to you"—was an emphatic declaration that framed the subsequent passage. He wished to assure these scholars that he was not merely issuing a formal acknowledgment of receipt of their letters. His joy at their correspondence was genuine.

To verify his awareness of their correspondence, he referred to both elements: "your letters and your questions." Although he had issued some disparaging remarks about the style of such compositions, he wished to assure them that he appreciated R. Jonathan's epistle as well as the twenty-four questions it accompanied.

The second instance in which this passage occurred was in Unit 10, right before his statement regarding his involvement in the competing intellectual world of *hokhmah*.

> And I, Moses, declare to the revered Rabbi, R. Jonathan the Kohen—and to all the scholars and their colleagues …that "before I was created in the womb the Torah selected me …. Nonetheless, "foreign women" became "Her rival-wives"….

Like the first declaration, this passage presaged an essential element of his *Iggeret*. But this declaration differed from the former in that Maimonides issued it to R. Jonathan as well as to the scholars who surrounded him.

Since this topic was supremely important, Maimonides made a point of expanding the audience for his announcement to include "all the scholars and their colleagues who will read my letter." As the final and most important element in Maimonides' extended apology, and as a vital summation of his distinctive intellectual worldview, he wanted to ensure that it would not be overlooked.

These two passages entailed the heart of his message to the Lunel scholars. The first declaration expressed his delight at the Lunel correspondence; the second presented an ideological justification for his delay, which was the competition for his intellectual attention demanded by "the other fields of knowledge." Of the various causes for his delayed response, Maimonides wished to emphasize—and acknowledge—the legitimate ideological tension within his soul that was a vital factor in his tardy response.

The second rhetorical device Maimonides used—also on two occasions and both within Unit 7—was the phrase, "I said to myself." Maimonides utilized this phrase to highlight key elements of his epistle. However, when Maimonides stated "I, Moses, declare," he followed that phrase with the main themes or messages of his letter. When he introduced passages with "I said to myself," he presented his own self-reflection upon the Lunel scholars and how he perceived their role in his life and legacy. In both instances when he used these words, a verse from Ruth chapter four followed.

> I said to myself, "Blessed be the Lord, who has not withheld a redeemer from you ..." (Ruth 4:14).

and

> I said to myself, "He [i.e., this scholar and community] will renew your life and sustain your old age" (Ruth 4:15).

In both of these passages, Maimonides advised the Lunel scholars that he wished to take them in his confidence by sharing with them his reflections and innermost thoughts about them. In the subsequent lines, he informed them that he considered them his "redeemers" and "sustainers."

One could argue that these generous and complimentary appellations were stock praises that Maimonides presented as formulaic tributes to his correspondents. However, another epistle Maimonides wrote that was addressed "To the Lunel Community"[117] demonstrated that his words in the *Iggeret* to R. Jonathan were to be taken literally.

Maimonides wrote that letter to the Lunel scholars shortly after he sent his responsum to R. Jonathan.[118] As in the *Iggeret* to R. Jonathan, Maimonides opened his letter to R. Jonathan's students with an apology for his delayed rejoinder. He advised them that he had sent a letter to Master Jonathan with his responses to all of their questions. He stated that he was enclosing with this letter to them the final book of the *Guide* as per their request, but in the original Arabic since he did not have time to translate it. He urged them to contact a local scholar, Samuel Ibn Tibbon, who could assist. He then added a remarkable challenge to the Lunel community of scholars:

> Now, you—my dear students and … —must strengthen and gird up yourselves, for I declare to you, that at this difficult time, the only men who remain to uphold the banner of Moses and to examine carefully the words of Ravina and Rav Ashi, are you and all the cities which surround you. For I know that you have set up study halls that are always open, and that you are individuals of understanding and wisdom [*hokhmah*].

Maimonides addressed these men as his "dear students" in language that was personal yet demanding. He introduced this segment with the header "I declare to you" to underscore the importance of these remarks. He graciously praised their dedication to intense Torah study in Lunel and "the [Provencal] cities which surround you,"[119] and depicted them as "individuals of understanding and *hokhmah*," reflecting their engagement in traditional learning as well as philosophy. Maimonides' first contact with the Lunel community was regarding astrology, and their urgent petition for a Hebrew version of his *Guide* further confirmed their interest in philosophy and "so many fields of knowledge." Since their intellectual interests resembled his own, he called them "my dear students."

This was followed by the main message of the letter regarding their unique role in the world of rabbinic scholarship. In the next lines, Maimonides reviewed the condition of Torah study in countries known to him, including Israel, Syria, and other nations of the East, Yemen, Arabia, and India.

> Whereas other places, the Torah has been lost to their descendants. Most of the major countries are deceased; a few of them are moribund; and approximately three or four places are ill. Regarding the countries in the West [Spain, and he probably included North Africa as well; i.e., those

countries where the Almohad invasion succeeded], it is well known what has been decreed against them, on account of our sinfulness.

He then proceeded to impose a historic responsibility on Provencal Jewry.

> Our sole remaining help is from you, our brothers, and our redeemers. Strengthen yourselves and we will be strengthened on behalf of our people. Endeavor to be men of valor because the matter depends upon you. Upon you is the decision—either release [the woman whose husband died without an heir] or perform the Levirate marriage.

> Do not depend upon my doing battle for I am, at this juncture, too old to go out to lead you to war. I have become very old and aged, not [merely] due to years but on account of the nature of the body. My illness is known. May the Blessed Creator help you in this regard, and may He designate you for fame and glory in the land. Amen.

This letter explicated some of the vital issues that plagued Maimonides at this time in his life. These concerns were not presented in his *Iggeret* to R. Jonathan since that letter was addressed to the elder scholar of the group. Maimonides' charge in this epistle was directed to R. Jonathan's pupils, the next generation of Provencal scholars. Here, Maimonides identified those men as the bearers of Jewish scholarship for the entire Jewish world: the "sole remaining help is from you.... the matter depends upon you. Upon you is the decision." With great clarity, Maimonides imposed upon these men the awesome responsibility to transmit the heritage of Jewish learning to the coming generations. They alone could uphold the "banner of Moses," which was to be understood as a double entendre: he placed upon their shoulders the transmission of the heritage of two Moseses—Moses, Our Teacher, and Moses, son of Maimon.

In the letter "To the Lunel Community," his opinion of these scholars was fully fleshed out in clear and direct language. It verified that Maimonides' effusive comments about them in his *Iggeret* to R. Jonathan were genuine. Although the rhetoric of the first part of his letter was in accord with the genre, he altered his style in the second half to convey his honest evaluation of his interlocutors. In accordance with his oft-stated compositional principles, he reverted back to the "perennial stream" of clear and precise language, verse citations as well as terminologies (such as "I, Moses, declare" and "I said to myself") to communicate his message to R. Jonathan and the Lunel community.

Maimonides drew heavily upon Ruth in both of his letters. In his *Iggeret* to R. Jonathan, Maimonides appropriated two verses from Ruth 4: "I said to myself, 'Blessed be the Lord, who has not withheld a redeemer from you....'" (verse 14) and "I said to myself, 'He will renew your life and sustain your old age" (verse 15). The central theme of Ruth was Naomi's life to death struggles. Will this grand-dame from Judea be able to survive after a decade in Moab and after her family members have passed on? When fate (God) enabled Ruth to encounter a "gibbor hayil" ("man of substance," Ruth 2:1), Naomi dared to hope anew. However, even after Naomi and Ruth had taken active and decisive steps to alter their personal fate, they both were dependent upon others to determine and secure their future.

In his "Letter to the Lunel Community" Maimonides compared the role of these scholars vis-à-vis the Jewish future to that of the redeemer in Ruth, Chapter 3. Like the redeemer, these men must decide whether to marry the childless woman—and sustain Israel's future—or release themselves from this role.

Maimonides adopted images and terminologies from Naomi's story as a parallel to his own life's circumstances as well as to the future of the Jewish community of his age. His repeated utilization of Ruth in his letters to the Lunel scholars provides the key to understanding the *Iggeret*, its historic meaning in the waning years of the Great Master as well as its compositional structure.

The *Iggeret* to R. Jonathan together with the "Letter to the Lunel Community" jointly preserve a portrait of Moses, son of Maimon, in his elder years. He had delivered his Law to his people and led them for decades. In both letters he declared, in direct and honest words, that his age and health did not allow him to lead as in previous years. Maimonides looked beyond the epoch of the MT, the twenty-four questions, and the *Guide*. He focused upon the future of Torah scholarship and his future as the Teacher of Israel. Both depended upon scholars who would carry forth the banner of Torah and *hokhmah*, thereby sustaining the ideology of Moses, son of Maimon. The Lunel community, by its own declarations, understood deeply what his MT had accomplished and they entreated him in four letters to explain his teachings. Not only did they wish to understand his Great *Hibbur*, they pleaded for a Hebrew translation of the *Guide* and, when he did not produce one, they undertook it upon themselves to have the text translated so that coming generations would be able to learn from Maimonides' *hokhmah* as well as from his MT. Thus, the Lunel scholars themselves were already playing a historic role in the transmission of the teachings of their Great Master. In ideological and real ways, these men were his worthy successors.

Maimonides shifted from rhymed prose in his letter to R. Jonathan because, as Maimonides himself observed, the style of rhymed prose was obscure and full of riddles. He needed to use direct and unadorned language to communicate to R. Jonathan and the Lunel scholars his dependence on "great men such as you" who, like the redeemer of Naomi, must stand in the breach to transmit Torah to the coming generations. He needed "to declare" that his laudatory remarks about Provencal Jewry were not stylized rhetoric, in accordance with popular poetics, but an honest, historic assessment. Maimonides shifted his style so that his deeply felt fears about the survival of Torah scholarship—both his own and the entire enterprise—would be clearly understood by his heirs, the Provencal scholars.

Maimonides addressed in this historic epistle what was uppermost in his mind at this stage of his life. The heart of his epistle was his "declaration" to R. Jonathan and the Lunel scholars: "I said to myself, 'Blessed be the Lord, who has not withheld a redeemer from you...'" and "I said to myself, 'He will renew your life and sustain your old age.'" Maimonides invoked these ancient words in celebration with the biblical Naomi when *his* redeemers and successors had arrived.[120]

APPENDIX

As in any research project, I identified various sources and explored some issues that, for one reason or another, I did not include in my study. Some of these explorations were too interesting to be left out entirely, hence this Appendix, which contains the following:

> Maimonides' Complex Attitude toward Poetry (p. 58)
> A Possible Prototype for Maimonides' *Iggeret*: The Halevi/Migas Letter to Provence (p. 64)

Maimonides' Complex Attitude toward Poetry

If the letter by Al-Fayyumi found in the Geniza was, indeed, written to Maimonides, it presents an image of the Grand Rabbi as an author of beautiful poems. This seemed surprising given many negative remarks Maimonides made about poetry in many of his works.

In this section, I shall review six selections from his writings on this topic.[121] Although I will conclude that his remarks did not refer to rhymed prose compositions, his attitude toward poetry was complex.[122]

Maimonides' earliest treatment of poetry was contained in his *Commentary to the Mishna*.[123] The opening section of Mishnah *Sanhedrin*, Chapter 10 lists various individuals who will lose their share in the World to Come because of their deviant beliefs and/or behaviors. In the first Mishna, the opinion of Rabbi Akiva is cited that individuals who read texts that were outside the accepted cannon (lit., "external books") will also suffer that punishment. Rabbi Akiva did not identify these deviant texts. Maimonides opined that such books were the books of heretics, "also the works of Ben Sira … which have neither wisdom (*hokhmah*) or practical use; they are a waste of time of mere nonsense; similarly, those books popular with Arabs [Maimonides then refers to different historical records of kings, tribal ancestry, etc.] and books of poetry and other [books] similar to them which have neither *hokhmah* nor practical value; rather, they are merely a waste of time."[124]

Maimonides disparaged poetry as a "waste of time" since it was neither a "*hokhmah* nor a skill/text of real, practical value."[125] Maimonides, even in his early years, devalued books that were not serious scholarly compositions. Historical or cultural records, social commentary, and artistic musings were devoid of value, and their readers will suffer the same fate as those who study esoteric writings.

His position here is doubly extreme. Although poetry might not have the same instructive or inspirational value as serious scholarly tomes, it is quite a leap to include it with sectarian literature, which might encourage ideas or practices that violated Jewish law.[126] Reading poetry might be a "waste of time" but it is remarkable that Maimonides held that one would forsake the World to Come for such an infraction. Secondly, Maimonides here seems to extend his prohibition to all forms of poetry. Did that also include devotional compositions? If so, it would seem that he has assumed an extreme position.[127]

In his *Commentary to the Mishnah* to *Avot*, Maimonides offered a fuller treatment of this topic.[128] *Avot 1:16* lauded the virtue of silence and in his *Commentary* Maimonides evaluated various forms of speech that polluted society or the individual speaker. In the context of his commentary, he referred to the practice of reading poetry at weddings or banquets that some, including "important and devout members of our people," prohibited when the verses were in Arabic. However, they permitted poetry to be read if it had been composed in Hebrew. Maimonides considered this to be "absolute foolishness." The determining factor, he wrote, should not be "the language in which it was composed, but its content." Here, he offered a definition of prohibited poems: those "intended to stimulate lust, to praise it and to entice a person to it...." This is the "kind of speech that is to be rejected since it [seeks to] arouse and stimulate...."

Maimonides here defined the kind of poetry that was prohibited and he provided the rationale: it was a medium that sought to stimulate the erotic and base nature of listeners with tales of love, lust, and sensual pleasure. In this regard, he was probably reacting to the Hebrew poems of his age that—mimicking the Arab models—were full of such examples. Verse was composed in tribute to wine, women, and—in some cases—men lovers.[129]

Esoteric books sought to capture or pervert the mind of their readers; poetry sought to ensnare the heart, body, and soul. Both were prohibited.

In his *Commentary to the Mishnah,* Maimonides presented two different explanations for his position on poetry. In *Sanhedrin*, he prohibited poetry as a valueless literature, devoid of any scholarly or practical worth. In *Avot*, he condemned the genre due to the nature of its erotic content, which was probably in reaction to the compositions popular at that time, especially in the Spain of his youth.

In his middle and later years, he expanded his negative statements about poetry to include devotional poetry, even though such compositions were neither purposeless nor erotic.

A questioner asked Maimonides about the appropriateness of the practice of prayer service leaders who added *piyyutim* (liturgical poems) to the liturgy.[130] The questioner wrote that some of these compositions were fashioned by the cantors themselves; some were doxologies and others were in honor of a groom or the father of a new son on the occasion of a circumcision. The questioners also inquired about the proper place for these *piyyutim* within the service, assuming they were acceptable additions. The question was intelligently fashioned and demonstrated an appreciation of the nuances of Jewish law.

Maimonides responded in two short sentences: "It is best not to recite even a word of such poetry ("shir") within the prayer [service]. But if the populace insists on saying it—because ignorance/stupidity dominates—it should be recited prior to the blessings surrounding the Sh'ma prayer...."

Maimonides clearly prohibited the inclusion of *piyyutim*, but his strong opposition and disparaging words might have been regarding the inclusion and intrusion of a new prayer into the traditional liturgy. His comments might merely reflect his conservative attitude toward the composition of contemporary prayers and their placement within the normative liturgy. His strong objection was not because of the genre but to the notion of composing a text that would interrupt the liturgy that had been carefully and conceptually structured.

Another responsum on the same topic offers additional insight into Maimonides' position.[131] Some petitioners cited various Talmudic statements regarding the language and terminologies used in liturgy, including references to prayers that could be recited in translation. These sources seemed contradictory and some were unclear. They petitioned Maimonides to explain the sources.

Maimonides responded decisively: "It is forbidden to alter in any fashion the format of the blessings from what the rabbis established." The practices sanctioned in the sources the petitioners cited did not introduce new material to the liturgy but merely added to it,

> which is not like the "piyyutim" that add material including much that is not relative to the liturgy, as well as their rhymes and melodies, which convert the liturgy from the category of prayer to comedy. This is the most significant contributing factor to the lack of attentiveness [in prayer] and which brings the people to behave without seriousness [during prayer] since they perceive that these words being said are not obligatory. In addition to this, [they perceive that] these "piyyutim" are sometimes the compilations of poets not scholars, whose words [i.e., that of the scholars] would be appropriate to use as supplications and to become closer to God through them. They divert [them?] from the words composed by the prophets or those at the level or prophets....[132]

Maimonides distinguished between liturgy composed by poets ("*m'shorerim*"), and that which entailed a verse of scripture, a compilation based upon biblical passages, or a prayer composed by "those who were [almost] at the level of prophets," by which he meant the Men of the Great Assembly who compiled much of what became the standard liturgy. Maimonides did not identify the characteristics that distinguished the biblical and rabbinic prayers from the poetic formulations, but it is likely that the former were inspired words whereas the *piyyutim* were mere human craft. Maimonides argued that this difference was not lost on the congregants who, during the chanting of *piyyutim*, behaved accordingly. Even the people were aware that this was a new addition to the service as compared to the normative liturgy, which was constructed upon the bedrock of biblical passages and inspired rabbinic compilations. Rather than enhancing the worship of the congregation by such addenda, the new *piyyutim* detracted from the sanctity of the service.

Maimonides prohibited *piyyutim* from the service because "It is forbidden to alter in any fashion the format of the blessings from what the rabbis established" and because these poetic innovations lacked the inspiration and standing of the normative liturgy. The divine biblical word and inspired rabbinic prayers will always trump the poetry of the *payytan*, even if he be Judah Halevi.

This responsum recorded Maimonides' attitude toward liturgical innovation and the relative worth of poetic compositions compared to the sublime and holy liturgy of biblical and rabbinic origin. The overall thrust of his remarks and their tone illustrate that Maimonides did not regard poetry as an effective and valued medium of religious inspiration. However, in this responsum he did not prohibit poetry per se as a literary genre. He did not state that it was a "waste of time" or a simplistic or superficial literary expression. Although his negative view of poetry is iterated in his responsum, his remarks were based upon his attitude regarding liturgical innovation and the relative spiritual impoverishment of uninspired poets of devotional prayers.

In two passages in his *Guide*, Maimonides referred to or discussed poetry. In Book I, he again coupled poetry with history and identified them as superficial disciplines, as he did in his *Commentary* to *Sanhedrin* discussed above. He criticized those who read a scholarly or philosophical text "and … consider … that you understand a book … while glancing through it as you would glance through a historical work or a piece of poetry…."[133] He did not explain why he held that poetry and history warranted this dismissive comment. Maimonides may have considered history as a mere listing of events and poetry a superficial or subjective impression of reality. From his Aristotelian perspective, neither entailed a scientific or rational examination of ideas and issues. Both could be readily mastered after a quick read.

That was not the case with *hokhmah* or Torah. In Book I, Maimonides presented the advice of a philosopher regarding the proper methodology of study. "A student of his books should not … ascribe to him effrontery, temerity, and an excess of haste to speak of matters of which he had no knowledge…. In the same way we say that man should not hasten too much to accede to this great and sublime matter at the first try, without having made his soul undergo training in the sciences and the different kinds of knowledge, having truly improved his character, and having extinguished the desires and cravings engendered in him by his imagination."[134]

Shortly after this passage, he stated: "When … he has achieved and acquired knowledge of true and certain premises and has achieved knowledge of the rules of logic and inference and of the various ways of preserving himself from the errors of the mind, he then should engage in the investigation of this subject."

Maimonides' rational approach to study and the acquisition of true wisdom is clearly presented in these passages. In order to achieve understanding, one had to perfect one's mind and character and that process entailed the subjugation of one's physical desires and passions. Poetry could serve as an impediment to that preparation and, as such, it might militate against one's ability to study and master *hokhmah* or Torah. Isadore Twersky described "Maimonides' approach to the role of reason in religion" and "his distaste for various manifestations of popular religion. There is a passionate insistence upon the purity of method, not only the correctness of result. The procedure, the modality, the motive—all are intrinsically significant, and this unites the nature of his rejection of astrological practices, his attempt to maximize intention and inwardness, his indictment of poetry and hymnology, and his condemnation of *kalam* philosophy, and his quest for reasons for the commandments. The echoes and reverberations of the cognitive motif are uniformly loud and clear."[135]

Maimonides' aside in the *Guide* regarding the superficiality of poetry and history echoes his comment to Sanhedrin. In both these sources, poetry and history were dismissed not because of erotic or sensual qualities, but because they fail to comprehend the nature of things that can only be done by rational analysis, which entails much discipline, preparation, study, and sheer effort. Poetry is a flawed discipline; it offers a superficial view of a complex world.

But, what about poetry that is serious, thoughtful, and directed to or regarding God? Was there no middle ground where an inspired and thoughtful religious thinker might compose poetry that brought one closer to God?

Maimonides' most extended treatment of poetry was on this topic. Within his discussion of affirmative attributes of God,[136] Maimonides wrote that the only attributes that could be recited in prayer were those selected by the Men of the Great Assembly "who were prophets."[137] Any other reference to God, even if a given metaphor is contained in the Bible, cannot be stated.

> Thus what we do is not like what is done by the truly ignorant who spoke at great length and spent great efforts on prayers that they composed and on sermons that they compiled and through which they, in their opinion, came nearer to God. In these prayers and sermons they predicate of God qualitative attributions that, if predicated of a human individual, would

designate a deficiency in him. For they do not understand those sublime notions that are too strange for the intellects of the vulgar...."

And later he chastises:

...poets and preachers or such as think that what they speak is poetry, so that the utterances of some of them constitute an absolute denial of faith, while other utterances contain such rubbish and such perverse imaginings as to make men laugh when they hear them, on account of the nature of these utterances, and to make them weep when they consider that these utterances are applied to God....[138]

Maimonides reserved his harshest criticism for poetry composed in God's name. Although the intent of the *payytan* was to glorify the Almighty with edifying prosody, Maimonides was unrelenting: when poetry was composed about God in inappropriate ways, it was not merely a waste of time, it was blasphemy.[139]

Maimonides' negative attitude toward poetry was based upon various grounds, ranging from its lack of scholarly or practical value and its erotic/sensual subject matter to its blasphemous nature when God is the subject. His position on poetry was explicated quite clearly in the sources cited above.

None of his concerns obtain regarding rhymed prose in the context of correspondence between individuals. Maimonides' rhymed prose section within the *Iggeret* did not, of course, entail erotic passages, nor was it a superficial artistic expression devoid of scholarly content. Not only was the agenda of his epistle an academic one, the poetic sections of the letter contained none of the negative elements of the poetry Maimonides disdained. Indeed, as I have illustrated in detail above, a substantial proportion of Maimonides' rhymed prose was derived from biblical verse. The utilization of biblical passages as the medium of expression meant that such rhymed prose was built upon inspired words from Scripture. The features that defined Maimonides' *Iggeret* as rhymed prose distanced it from the kind of poetry Maimonides objected to in his various works and throughout his life.

A Possible Prototype for Maimonides' *Iggeret*: The Halevi/Migas Letter to Provence

I identified in this work texts that might have influenced Maimonides' epistle, such as his own prior composition to R. Anatoli and R. Jonathan's epistles to him. Another letter that might have influenced Maimonides was a rhymed prose epistle composed by Judah Halevi (before 1075–1141).

Halevi was one of the seminal figures in the flowering of medieval Hebrew poetry.[140] He composed a letter at the request of and in the name of R. Joseph Ibn Migas (Spain; 1077–1141) that—like Maimonides' *Iggeret*—was sent to French scholars. Spanish scholars focused exclusively on tractates of the Babylonian Talmud, which dealt with daily and contemporary life. Provencal scholars studied the entire Talmud and R. J. Ibn Migas wished to obtain a commentary on the Mishnah, Order *Kodashim* ("Holy Things"—dealing with sacrifices and the Temple rite) from the scholars of Narbonne.[141] This city was the earliest and most important center of scholarship in Provence,[142] and R. J. Ibn Migas petitioned Narbonne scholars since this commentary was not found in Spain.

This was an important request. R. J. Ibn Migas might have presumed that a letter composed by the renowned poet Halevi would be an effective means of gaining the attention and favor of the Narbonne community. Like Maimonides, Halevi had the distinction of enjoying during his lifetime the adulation of his people. By the first quarter of the twelfth century, he was well known and admired throughout the Jewish world,[143] and it seems likely that he composed his epistle around that period. Thus, it was written around three-quarters of a century before Maimonides' *Iggeret* to R. Jonathan. It is also possible that R. J. Ibn Migas was insufficiently skilled in rhymed prose, thus he hired a professional writer to compose a proper epistle, which was a common practice in both Arab and Jewish societies.

The R. J. Ibn Migas epistle began with a brief poem before the rhymed prose text. In the rhymed prose section, he called the Narbonne scholars "mighty Torah warriors" and "redeemers of the Diaspora." As I noted above regarding Maimonides' two letters, the first metaphor occurs frequently in Talmudic passages regarding scholars.[144]

In the next two units, R. J. Ibn Migas offered a prayer for the well-being of his honored recipients and apologized for communicating with them in writing: "If I had wings like a dove I would fly [to you]." He referred to a "precious" letter he had received from them that touched him deeply. He devoted a number of lines in praise of their letter including an adaptation of a verse in *Song of Songs* (6:10).[145] Maimonides used the same verse in a letter to the community of Lunel (not the *Iggeret* to R. Jonathan) decades later. R. J. Ibn Migas then apologized that the distance between them and the lack of time impeded his ability to visit them in person.

In the next part of the letter, he entreated the scholars of Narbonne to send him a copy of the Commentary to *Kodashim* and assured them that he would send the fee for the transcriber. He concluded the letter with prayers for their well-being.

The R. J. Ibn Migas epistle comprised five units, each serving a specific function in the development of the composition:

1. *Opening tribute and prayer:* R. J. Ibn Migas preceded his letter with a poem, followed by rhymed prose that offered praise for his recipients and prayers for their well-being;
2. *Review/tribute of prior letters:* R. J. Ibn Migas lauded a letter he had received from Narbonne that brought him much pleasure;
3. *Apology:* R. J. Ibn Migas apologized for the medium of communication—that is, a written text—and his inability to present his request and message in person;
4. *The core of the epistle:* the main body of the letter and its objective, which was the request for the Mishnah commentary;
5. *Salutation and final blessing.*[146]

In addition to sharing similar formal structure, the Maimonides and Halevi epistles shared similar background and purpose. Both letters were composed by a noted Sephardic figure to a circle of Provencal scholars. In both instances, neither author had an established or long-standing relationship with his correspondents. In fact, the R. J. Ibn Migas–Narbonne exchange is the earliest known literary connection between scholars of these two communities.[147] Most important, the purpose of both correspondences was essentially the same. Both were regarding texts—Maimonides' MT and *Guide*, or a Mishnah commentary on *Kodashim*—which each party regarded highly; and, in both cases, the text was sent from one to the other as a result of the initial letter.

This rhymed prose composition had been written to an earlier generation of Provencal scholars with the same objective as Maimonides' epistle to R. Jonathan and the Lunel circle. Given its similar agenda and the community that it addressed, it would have been a treasured precedent.

There was one other element of this epistle that would have earned Maimonides' rapt attention, and that was its signatory: R. J. Ibn Migas. Anything written by him or in his name would have engaged Maimonides because of the decisive role R. J. Ibn Migas played in Maimonides' scholarly development, directly and indirectly.

R. J. Ibn Migas had studied under R. Isaac Alfasi (1013–1103) at his famous academy in Lucena (Spain). Some biographical sketches of Halevi state that he, too, had studied at Lucena. If those sketches are correct, that would make him a classmate of R. J. Ibn Migas.[148] R. J. Ibn Migas succeeded R. Alfasi as Head of the Academy and one of his students was Maimon, Maimonides' father. (Interestingly, according to some scholars, R. Jonathan of Lunel also attended the academy at Lucena, where he studied under R. J. Ibn Migas's son, Meir, who succeeded his father.)[149]

Maimonides revered both Lucena Masters and in his MT he called them his teachers: "Thus my Masters ruled—Rav Yosef Halevi and his Master [i.e., Alfasi], of blessed memory."[150] In the Introduction to his *Commentary to the Mishnah*, he noted that he disagreed with Alfasi's decisions "less than ten times"[151] and in a responsum he corrected that number to "around thirty instances."[152]

Right after his tribute to Alfasi in his Mishnah Introduction (cited above), Maimonides paid homage to R. J. Ibn Migas as the "king, after whom no one would follow." He described how he treasured R. J. Ibn Migas's works:

> I collected all that happened to come into my hand from the glosses of my father ... and others, in the name of R. Joseph [R. J. Ibn Migas]. I testify that that man's understanding of the Talmud astounds everyone who takes note of his statements and the profundity of his perception....[153]

Given Maimonides' laudatory remarks about R. J. Ibn Migas and his reference to him as one of his Masters, some scholars incorrectly assumed that he had actually studied under him as his student.[154]

Although Maimonides' relationship to R. J. Ibn Migas as a disciple was academic and not actual, a letter written in his name to the Provencal scholars would have been sought out as a great treasure. Maimonides would not have considered R. J. Ibn Migas's correspondence as valued as his Talmud commentaries, but he would not have failed to take note of it, especially given its similar agenda and destination.

As I noted above, it is also possible that the structural similarity between these letters was due to the fact that they were both written in accordance with the conventions of rhymed prose epistles. Their formal resemblance might merely reflect their respective compliance with the norms of epistolary composition. However, given the similar objective of these two letters and, in particular, the name of the signatory of the epistle, it is tantalizing to consider whether the Halevi/R. J. Ibn Migas letter played a role in the development of Maimonides' *Iggeret* to R. Jonathan.

I was unable to find any source—literary or historic—indicating that Maimonides was aware of the Halevi/R. J. Ibn Migas epistle or if he even knew of its existence. Additionally, I did not find any testimony that the Ibn Migas epistle circulated in Maimonides' time as an independent document under his name. It has come down to us within the collected writings of Judah Halevi; its fame was because of its author, not its signatory. The only way this composition could have influenced Maimonides' writing was if he was aware of Halevi and his oeuvre, and had encountered this letter within a collection of Halevi's writings. The question of the possible influence of this earlier epistle on Maimonides, then, depends on the extent to which Maimonides was knowledgeable of Halevi's writings in general, which is a question that goes beyond this work.

Endnotes

1   See note 10.
2   All references in this study to Prof. Decter will be to his forthcoming book. Since the pagination of his book is not final, citations from *Dominion Built of Praise* will be to the chapter only.
3   Although the MT was disseminated by Maimonides in the late 1170s, he revised the text throughout his life, as is evident from many of his later writings (see below), and a date cannot be identified by which time it became a final product.
    In three places in the MT, Maimonides provided the year during which that unit of the MT was being written. In each instance, he noted the number of years that had passed since the Destruction of the Temple in 70 CE. In the *Introduction* to the MT, he wrote that the year was "1108 years after the Destruction," which would be 1178/9; in *Laws of Sabbatical and Jubilee Years* 10:4, he listed the year as "4936, which was 1107 years after the Destruction," which would be 1177; in *Laws of Consecration of the New Moon* 11:16, he wrote that the year was "4938, which was 1109 years after the Destruction," which would be 1179. See Isadore Twersky, *Introduction to the Code of Maimonides (Mishneh Torah)* (New Haven, CT: Yale University Press, 1982), 518, who states that MT was "completed in 1178, or possibly 1180...."
4   See note 23 regarding the arrival of the MT in Provence. See I. Sonne, "Maimonides' Letter to Samuel Ibn Tibbon" [in Hebrew], *Tarbiz* 10, 2 (1939), 146–47, especially his chronology of Maimonides' works.
5   See B. Z. Benedict, "On the History of the Torah-Centre in Provence," *Tarbiz* 22, 2 (January, 1951), 85–109.
6   The Lunel correspondence is generally called the "Twenty-Four Questions" since the questions were organized into 24 separate letters. However, Letters 286 and 289 contain three and two questions, respectively, so that the actual total is 27.
7   Herbert Davidson (*Maimonides: The Man and His Works* [New York, Oxford University Press, 2005], 291) concluded that only 65 of the responsa—which he numbered as 480—dealt with "purely theoretical questions"; the twenty-four from Lunel are included in that total.
8   See his remarks in *Milhamot Ha-Shem*, Reuven Margaliot, ed. (Jerusalem: Mossad Harav Kook; n.d.), 52–53. Rabbi Yosef Qafih, however, held that the twenty-four responsa to these scholars attributed to Maimonides were forgeries. See his "The Questions from the Scholars of Lunel and the Responsa of the Rambam; Are They Authentic?" [in Hebrew] in the *Rabbi Y. Nissim Memorial Book*, vol. 11 (Jerusalem, n.p., 1985), 235–52 and the response of R. I. Shailat, which follows in this volume.

9   For example, see standard MT commentaries to Laws of Slaughter 8:14, Laws of Forbidden Foods 11:18, and Vows 12:1. Note especially that *Migdal Oz* consistently cites the Lunel correspondence in his commentary.

10 It should be noted that, compared to Maimonides' major works—the *Commentary on the Mishna, Mishneh Torah,* and *Guide for the Perplexed*—which have generated centuries of scholarship, Maimonides' responsa have been relatively neglected. These letters were written over four decades to scholars and communities the world over. However, since most were composed in Arabic, they were accessible only to those who knew the language.

A modest anthology of 150 responsa, entitled *P'er Ha-Dor*, was translated and published by R. Mordecai Tammah in Amsterdam in 1765. But it was not until 1957 to 1961 when Prof. Joshua Blau issued a three-volume edition of Maimonides' responsa in original and translation (*Teshuvot ha-Rambam* [*Responsa*], 3 volumes, translated into Hebrew by Joshua Blau [Jerusalem, Mekitze Nirdamim, 1957-1961])—and in 1989, he added a fourth volume—that Maimonides' full correspondence was made available to the scholarly world. Until a few decades ago, a large proportion of writings by Maimonides was inaccessible to most students of Jewish tradition.

In general, Maimonides' responsa were terse, brief rejoinders. In a few lines, he rendered his decision or approval/disapproval of a position the petitioner had presented, and he did not always provide full textual supports for his answer. The Lunel rejoinders, on the other hand, received a more robust response from the Great Master. His admiration of these petitioners and his appreciation of their challenge—as he himself said, as will be cited in this study—warranted fuller treatment.

11 A quick examination of the commentaries to the Rabbinic Bible (*Mikra'ot G'dolot*) as well as many collections of responsa and Talmud commentaries, will illustrate the ubiquity of this kind of poetic composition.

12 See Twersky, *Introduction to the Code*, 324-55, who reviews the intentional choices that Maimonides made regarding the language and literary style of his compositions.

13 Leon D. Stitskin, "Maimonides's Last Two Recorded Letters," *Tradition* 15 (1975): 186-192. Following the epistle to R. Jonathan, Stitskin presented "Maimonides's Letter to the Leaders of Lunel." Stitskin subsequently included these letters in his *Letters of Maimonides* (New York: Yeshiva University Press, 1977), 159-162.

14 Twersky, *Introduction to the Code*, 37-41, of which half entails an introduction to the letter. Twersky noted that the first draft of the translation was prepared by his student, David Stern.

15 Interestingly, neither scholar informed the reader—either in his introduction or footnotes—that his translated text represented only one-half of the epistle.

16 See Alexander Marx, "The Correspondence between the Rabbis of Southern France and Maimonides about Astrology," *Hebrew Union College Annual* 3 (1926): 311-58. Marx published this letter from a manuscript in the library of the Jewish Theological Seminary, together with an introduction and Maimonides' responsum to them.

Itzhak Shailat published Maimonides' responsum to the Southern France scholars in *Iggrot ha-Rambam* (*The Letters and Essays of Moses Maimonides*) (Jerusalem: Shailat Publishing-Ma'aleh Adumim, 5755/1995), vol. II, 478-490, based upon various editions, some of which were not available to Marx; see also his introduction to the letter (474-77). Maimonides' letter was translated by Ralph Lerner in *Medieval Political Philosophy: A Sourcebook*, ed. Ralph Lerner and Muhsin Mahdi (Ithaca, NY: Cornell University Press, 1963), 227-36. Quotations are from his translation.

17 Especially Shabbat 156a/b.

18 Marx, "The Correspondence," 347, line 9.
19 See Shailat, *Iggrot ha-Rambam,* vol. II, 491–92. Marx, "The Correspondence," 333, states that R. Jonathan was "the center and moving spirit of the circle of scholars who addressed themselves to Maimonides."

   Davidson, *Maimonides,* 494, note 35: "When R. Jonathan later wrote to Maimonides, he made clear that he represented a circle of scholars in Lunel. Montpellier and Lunel both lie between Narbonne and Marseilles, and they are only about twenty miles apart. The authors of the letter to Maimonides may possibly have thought that it would be easier for the messenger carrying Maimonides' reply to deliver it to Montpellier than to Lunel; or perhaps R. Jonathan changed his place of residence from one town to the other in the interval; or, a third alternative, the place name that has been corrupted in the manuscript may, in fact, be Lunel." See also Davidson, *Maimonides,* 494, note 36, regarding I. Sonne's discussion in *Tarbiz* 10.
20 Blau, *Teshuvot ha-Rambam,* vol. III, 53. In the original, there is a sequence of passages (all in rich poetic language) that, to this reader, were unquestionable references by R. Jonathan to Maimonides' responsum in which he rejected astrology. It is surprising that Marx, citing those passages in Maimonides' *Iggeret,* wrote: "*Perhaps* [my emphasis] the statement in the letter … refers to this point" (Marx, "The Correspondence," 323, note 19).
21 Marx, *The Correspondence,* 323. Actually, in the final paragraph of their letter, the French scholars explained how they came to know about Maimonides and what stimulated their inquiry to him. They reported that "a composition regarding the coming of the Messiah … was brought to our country—which was stated in your name—regarding … a distant land … where a prophet had arisen within Israel who spoke about the coming of the Redeemer. You informed the men of Fez regarding this matter.…" The scholars were apparently impressed at the manner in which Maimonides had handled this difficult religious and communal matter. They stated that this composition that they obtained purely by accident inspired them to submit their astrological dilemma to his sensitive and knowledgeable judgment. They were silent about his great MT and philosophical *magnum opus* because these works had not yet reached Provence. Instead, a modest tome—which Maimonides identified in his responsum as a letter he had composed twenty-two years earlier to Yemen (not to Fez, as stated in their letter)—brought about an association between the Jews of Provence and Maimonides that ultimately enabled a correspondence that earned an important niche in the history of halakhic correspondence.

   If it was Maimonides' letter to Yemen that attracted these scholars to consult with him regarding astrology, what prompted Maimonides—albeit, belatedly—to respond to them? Given his overwhelming responsibilities as court physician—a theme that appears in almost all of his later letters, as will be discussed below—what brought him to assume the role of rabbinic decisor and master teacher even to far-flung communities in Christian Europe?

   In his response to the Jews of Montpellier regarding astrology, Maimonides himself explained what moved him to respond to their appeal. He stated:

   > The Lord knows that, were it not for the fact that Rabbi Phinehas had sent a messenger who pressed [me until I was too] embarrassed [to resist], and who didn't leave me until I wrote the letter, I would not have responded at this time because I do not have free time. (Shailat, *Iggrot ha-Rambam,* vol. II, 490)

With surprising candor, Maimonides declared that his response "at this time" was not out of respect for the honorable and learned scholars of Montpellier, but due to the personal intercession by a scholar he could not refuse. Rabbi Phinehas was a rabbi from Provence who had settled in Alexandria and received an appointment there as judge, possibly upon the recommendation of Maimonides. Various letters between the two scholars have survived, including a famous critique of MT by this Alexandrian judge. From their correspondence it is clear that their relationship was a difficult one (see Shailat, *Iggrot ha-Rambam*, vol. II, 433–54, including his introduction and notes).

We may surmise that R. Phinehas had received an appeal from his former compatriots to intercede on their behalf with the Grand Rabbi of Cairo. Maimonides himself admitted that R. Phinehas' persistent and embarrassing pressure was instrumental in stimulating his response. His connection with Provence might never have occurred were it not for the presence of a French agent in Egypt.

Given R. Phinehas' letter to Maimonides regarding his MT and other matters, he was obviously aware of Maimonides' great scholarship. He could have provided his Provencal colleagues with a review of Maimonides' remarkable knowledge and he could have been the party who encouraged them at the outset to address their question about astrology to him. However, there is no evidence that he played that role.

As I noted above, the French rabbis seem ignorant of Maimonides' works and they themselves stated that they contacted him on their own based upon their impression of his learning as evidenced in his letter to Fez/Yemen. Had R. Phinehas played a role in directing them to Maimonides, they would have stated it.

22 Re Maimonides' usage of the term "West"—*ma'arab* in Hebrew and *maghrib* in Arabic—see Davidson, *Maimonides*, 24 and note 84, in which he cites Goitein and Blau to suggest "a broad sense of the term" to include Spain as well as North Africa.

23 I. Twersky (*Introduction to the Code*, 518), based upon this correspondence, states regarding the dissemination of MT that it first reached the "Oriental countries (Palestine, Syria, Babylon [Iraq], Yemen), then ... the Mediterranean area (including Spain and Provence), and finally ... the Franco-German orbit as well. By 1191 Maimonides spoke of its renown in all corners of the earth, even though in 1193 it had apparently not yet reached southern France. By the turn of the century it was firmly rooted in the Provencal-Castile region and was the subject of intense study."

See, however, Shailat, *Iggrot ha-Rambam*, vol. II, 474–76 (especially note 3), who offers a different opinion regarding the date by which the MT had reached Provence. He posits that Maimonides stated his remarks to the French enquirers regarding astrology tongue-in-check, upbraiding them for not carefully mastering his MT. Shailat concludes that "it seems appropriate to establish that MT reached Lunel not later than 1193."

24 Shailat, *Iggrot ha-Rambam*, vol. II, 474.

25 In Responsum 345, for example, the scholars of Lunel note that Maimonides' position on a given point is stated in various places in the MT as well as "in other works." Their familiarity—and mastery—of his works is evidenced from their questions.

26 The letter from R. Jonathan is in Blau, *Teshuvot ha-Rambam*, vol. III, 49–54. The letter by Maimonides to the community of Lunel is in Shailat, *Iggrot ha-Rambam*, vol. II, 557–59.

The sequencing of the four Lunel letters has been established by Samuel Miklos Stern, "The Correspondence between Maimonides and the Scholars of Provence" [in Hebrew], *Zion* XVI (1951): 18–29. See also his "Autographs of Maimonides in the Bodleian Library," in *Medieval Arabic and Hebrew Thought*, ed. F. W. Zimmermann

(London: Variorum Reprints, 1983), 194–202, reprinted from the Bodleian Library Record V (Oxford, 1955). See also Shailat, *Iggrot ha-Rambam*, vol. II, 491–98.

The convincing work of S. Stern regarding the sequence and timing of the four letters demonstrated that Maimonides' delay to the first inquiry regarding astrology was not because "he had not formed a very high opinion of the writers," as Marx suggested ("The Correspondence," 326–27). Despite his declared admiration for the twenty-four questions, he did not respond any more promptly to that second Provencal inquiry. In his *Iggeret* to R. Jonathan, he presented various reasons for his delay and, assumedly, those causes obtained in both exchanges with the French rabbis.

27 This date is found in a manuscript (Paris 416) at the conclusion of Maimonides' response to the twenty-four questions (Blau, *Teshuvot ha-Rambam*, vol. III, 29, 42). Blau dates this manuscript to the fifteenth century. It contains the twenty-four questions but not the *Iggeret*.
28 Blau, *Teshuvot ha-Rambam*, vol. III, 55–57.
29 Shailat, *Iggrot ha-Rambam*, vol. II, 499–503.
30 JPS: *Hebrew-English Tanakh* (Philadelphia: The Jewish Publication Society, 1999), 990, note a: "Meaning of Hebrew uncertain; emendation yields 'striding.'"
31 Both Blau and Shailat note that the different manuscripts use one or another of these nouns, either emphasizing the scholarly character of R. Jonathan or his elevated status as a Kohen.
32 Blau (*Teshuvot ha-Rambam*, vol. III, 55, lines 8–9) here follows MSS Paris 181, which has "priests," as found in Isaiah 61:6. Shailat (*Iggrot ha-Rambam*, vol. II, 499, line 12; see note 13) cites the Simonson edition, which has the more generic term "people" here.
33 JPS *Tanakh*, 584; and see there note *a-a*, "Meaning of Hebrew uncertain."
34 Ibid., 623; and see there note *f-f*, "...but meaning of Hebrew uncertain."
35 In the *Iggeret*, the two clauses of this verse in Samuel were reversed to sustain the rhyme.
36 The translation here is that of the JPS *Tanakh*. In the context of the letter, however, "g'vurah" might be understood as in Ecclesiastes 10:17, in the sense of restraint. Maimonides, while acknowledging the strength of their questions "which had not been heard," also notes the nobility and gallantry of their challenge to his MT.
37 In medieval Hebrew, terms such as "mashal ve-hidda" or "mashal u-melitza" designated a passage as a fictional or narrative passage or, simply—as in this instance ("divrei ha-hidot ve-ha'mshalim")—rhymed prose. See Rina Drory, *Models and Contracts—Arabic Literature and Its Impact on Medieval Jewish Culture* (Leiden, The Netherlands: Brill, 2000), 226, note 22. At this point in his epistle, Maimonides characterized the stylistic guidelines of the genre that defined his composition up to this point and he indicated that he wished to continue in a different register.
38 Blau (*Teshuvot ha-Rambam*, vol. III, 56, note 40) cites a manuscript that has the words "as of today" at this point.
39 See Shailat, *Iggrot ha-Rambam*, vol. II, 502, note 62, which discusses the reference to "letters."
40 Blau's version of the *Iggeret* (cited above in note 30) adds "and because of the needs of those who pester me at all times," which is probably another reference to his many patients, as in Unit 8 of the *Iggeret*.
41 Blau (*Teshuvot ha-Rambam*, vol. III, 57; see note 62) cites here the incorrect addition (in MSS Paris 181) of the word "very," which does not appear here in the book of Esther.

42 I will focus on the latter two rhetorical elements—Maimonides' language and his utilization of biblical verse. Issues such as rhyme and, in general, poetics go beyond the scope and purpose of this study.
43 S. M. Stern translated a letter written by R. Jonathan. Regarding the translation of biblical passages in the letter, he observed: "One must know one's Bible well to appreciate—or even to understand—the letter. It was clearly impossible to give here a full annotation (which would mainly consist in references to the biblical passages alluded to), so that the reader will probably feel out of his depth at this or that phrase. I shall explain some of the most difficult passages." ("Autographs of Maimonides," 196, note 1.)
44 *Encyclopedia Judaica* (Jerusalem: Keter Publishing, 1972), vol. 13, 683.
45 Referring to praise texts discovered in the Cairo Geniza, in S. D. Goitein's *A Mediterranean Society: The Jewish Communities of the Arab World as Portrayed in the Documents of the Cairo Geniza* (Oakland: University of California Press, 2000), 5:35, cited by Decter, *Dominion Built of Praise*, introduction. [Goitein's 6-volume work was originally published between 1967 and 1993.]
46 Decter (*Dominion Built of Praise*, chap. 1) is quoting Thomas Blount, writing in 1656. Decter also questions Jefim Schirmann's position, that Iberian panegyrics was the outgrowth of the poet's dependence on his patron ("The Function of the Hebrew Poet in Medieval Spain," *Jewish Social Studies* 16, no. 3 [July 1954], 236). Decter views this style as emerging more broadly. Maimonides' effusive praise to his Lunel correspondents, who surely were not his patrons, sustains Decter's position.
47 Decter, *Dominion Built of Praise*, Introduction.
48 Decter, ibid., notes that when Maimonides corresponded with the Jewish community in Yemen, whose leader Maimonides had never met, he addressed his letter "To the Honored, great, and holy master and teacher … wise and kind, beloved and respected sage, son of the honored, great, and holy master and teacher … distinguished prince of Yemen, etc."
49 Ibid.
50 See Louis Ginzberg, *Legends of the Jews* (Philadelphia: Jewish Publication Society, 1968), vol. V, 272, note 19.
51 See Shailat, *Iggrot ha-Rambam*, vol. I, 223, line 8.
52 Interestingly, Maimonides did not use the famous passage in Malachi (chap. 2: 1, 6–7) which outlined the teaching role of the Kohen in ancient Israel: "And now, O priests, this charge is for you…. Proper rulings were in his mouth, / And nothing perverse was on his lips; / He served Me with complete loyalty / And held the many back from iniquity. / For the lips of a priest guard knowledge, / And men seek rulings from his mouth; / For he is a messenger of the Lord of Hosts." He may have avoided this passage since it was, in fact, an indictment of the Kohanim for having "turned away from that course; You have made the many stumble through your rulings; you have corrupted the covenant of the Levites…" (verses 8–9).
53 Decter, *Dominion Built of Praise*, chap. 1.
54 Ibid. Decter notes that "there are no manuals for Hebrew letter writing on the scale of the Arabic guides for scribes, there do survive Geniza manuscripts that compile Hebrew literary introductions for letters to addressees, both real and hypothetical, of various ranks (gaon, scribe, cantor, even synagogue caretaker), thus following the structural organization of Arabic epistolary manuals."
55 Shailat, *Iggrot ha-Rambam*, vol. II, 500, note 39.

56 Maimonides reversed the words in Deuteronomy 32:36—from "neither bond nor free is left" to "neither free nor bond is left"—so that the final syllable in this line would rhyme with the next passage.
57 See Jeffrey H. Tigay, *The JPS Torah Commentary, Deuteronomy* (Philadelphia: The Jewish Publication Society, 1996), 312.
58 See Drory, *Models and Contracts*, who documents and interprets this cultural development in Eastern and Western Jewish societies. See also Yosef Tobi, *Proximity and Distance; Medieval Hebrew and Arabic Poetry*, trans. Murray Rosovsky (Leiden, The Netherlands: Brill, 2003) especially chap. 9 ("Metaphor in Hebrew Medieval Poetry") and chap. 12 ("Aristotle's 'Poetics' in Medieval Jewish Literature").
59 Drory, *Models and Contracts*, 191–92: "…the picture seems quite clear: Dumas ben Labrat adopts Arab metrics; the adherents of his rival, Menachem ben Saruq, denounce Dunas for his borrowing…."
60 An uneducated Baghdadi Jew, Joseph Ibn Gabir (Shailat, *Iggrot ha-Rambam*, vol. I, 409), wrote to Maimonides about his difficulty with the MT since he did not know Hebrew, and appealed to him to issue an Arabic translation. In Maimonides' touching response, he urged Joseph to work his way through the Hebrew original "because it is easy to understand and very accessible. After you become accustomed to one section of it, you will [be able to] understand the rest of the 'Hibbur.'"

R. Jacob Emden (d. 1776) offered the following tribute regarding Maimonides' clarity of language in his works: "…Maimonides' wording … is ten times finer and clearer than the wording of all the treatise writers in Israel since the conclusion of the Talmud." *Lehem Shamayim* to Pe'ah 7:2, as cited by Isadore Twersky, "Some Reflections on the Historical Image of Maimonides; An Essay on His Unique Place in Jewish History," in *The Legacy of Maimonides: Religion, Reason and Community*, eds. Yamin Levy and Shalom Carmy (Brooklyn: Yashar Books, 2006), 7.
61 Twersky, "Some Reflections on the Historical Image," 33. In his *Introduction to the Code*, Prof. Twersky wrote the following regarding the MT (page 325): "Maimonides … sought a language suitable to his literary-pedagogic aims of reformulating the totality of Halakhah for the entire Jewish people, that (a) would be readily intelligible to the greatest number of readers; (b) would be flexible, rich and expressive; and (c) would enable him to write with precision, brevity, and elegance."
62 Decter, *Dominion Built of Praise*, chap. 1.
63 Maimonides' position on poetry is so well known that, whenever I shared with colleagues that I was working on a rhymed prose epistle by Maimonides and was perplexed by his sudden style reversal, every one of them—without exception—responded that it probably had something to do with his negative attitude toward poetry.
64 Heinrich Graetz, "Zenith of the Spanish-Jewish Culture; Jehuda Halevi," in *History of the Jews*, vol. III (Philadelphia: Jewish Publication Society, 1967), 317.
65 Jacob Mann, *The Jews in Egypt and in Palestine under the Fāṭimid Caliphs*, vol. II (London: Oxford University Press, 1920–22, reprinted 1970), 315–16.
66 Davidson, *Maimonides*, 37, note 146, citing Jacob Mann, *The Jews in Egypt*, vol. II, 319. See also Shailat, *Iggrot ha-Rambam*, vol I, 423.
67 Mann, *The Jews in Egypt*, vol. I, 244.
68 Ibid., vol. II, 315–16.
69 See Shailat, *Iggrot ha-Rambam*, vol. II, 468–70, for the letter and Shailat's introduction to the epistle (465–66), in which he discusses R. Anatoli's dates and the correspondence between him and Maimonides. Blau, *Teshuvot ha-Rambam*,

vol. II, 620–23, Responsum 346 is a rather lengthy exchange between these men. The concluding remarks by Maimonides record his high regard for R. Anatoli's scholarship and presence in Alexandria. R. Anatoli is also known from his halakhic exchanges with Maimonides' son, Abraham. In one letter to him, R. Abraham addressed him as "The scholar of our generation." As cited in Shailat, *Iggrot ha-Rambam*, vol. II, 466.

70 The sudden shift from benevolent and honored guest to potential combatant in both letters bears some resemblance to Spanish Hebrew poetic styles that were derived from Arabic models. The Arabic genre called "maqama" often entailed surprise reversals or revelations about characters within the poem. (See Rina Drory, "The Maqama" in *The Literature of Al-Andalus*, eds. Maria Menocal, Raymond Scheindlin, and Michael Sells [Cambridge: Cambridge University Press, 2000], 190–210.) Maimonides could be following this style in these two letters.

71 See Davidson, *Maimonides*, 70.

72 See note 26, above.

73 A photograph of the original document (Oxford 2874) is found in Shailat *Iggrot ha-Rambam*, vol. II, 498. Two photographs of parts of this MSS are found in Stern, "Autographs of Maimonides" (see note 26, above). In that article, he also translated the epistle.

74 Shailat is correct in his rejection (*Iggrot ha-Rambam*, vol. II, 494, note 9) of Stern's suggestion (p. 199 in his "Autographs of Maimonides"; see note 26, above) that this was a note to Maimonides' secretary. The main purpose of the note was its second part, which was to remind himself to complete his responsa to the Lunel group. That task could not be assigned to his assistant.

75 See note 26, above.

76 Stern, "Autographs of Maimonides," 196, no. 3.

77 S. M. Stern suggests in "The Correspondence" (p. 18) that Judah Al-Harizi (1170–1235) could have composed this poem at R. Jonathan's request given its style and because he had visited Provence around that time. However, according to Aharon Mirsky (*Encyclopedia Judaica*, vol. 2, 627), Al-Harizi "visited Provence, returning to Spain in 1190…," which means he was not in Provence in the mid-1190s when the Lunel correspondence was composed.

78 Blau, *Teshuvot ha-Rambam*, vol. III, 49–54. Blau's version is based upon MSS Paris no. 181. On p. 49, he lists other variants that he cited in his notes.

79 See Nahum M. Sarna, *Exploring Exodus: The Heritage of Biblical Israel* (New York: Schocken Books, 1986), 32; and *JPS: Hebrew-English Tanakh*, 115, note *a* (Heb. Mosheh from Egyptian for "born of"; here associated with mashah 'draw out.')

80 See note 66, above.

81 Blau, *Teshuvot ha-Rambam*, vol. III, 50, line 23. Maimonides' citation of the verse is in ibid., 55, line 5.

82 Ibid., vol. III, 50, lines 19–20.

83 Stern, "Autographs of Maimonides," 196.

84 Blau, *Teshuvot ha-Rambam*, vol. III, 52–53.

85 Decter (*Dominion Built of Praise*, chap. 5—"A Word Aptly Spoken": The Ethics of Praise) discusses the theological and moral implications of the excesses of panegyrics. He does not evaluate the ethics of scriptural adaptation.

86 David Hartwig (Tsevi) Baneth, *Iggrot ha-Rambam* (Jerusalem: Magnes Press, 1985; reprint of 1946 edition), 10.

87 When I started my research on this project, Prof. Raymond Scheindlin (Jewish Theological Seminary) informed me (private communication) that a full scholarly analysis of medieval epistolary style had not been undertaken.
88 Dector, *Dominion Built of Praise*, chap. 1.
89 R. Abraham, son of Maimon, wrote the following regarding the Lunel questions: "These compositions of my father and Master—may the memory of the righteous be a blessing—the Great Composition that he composed in the Holy Tongue (Hebrew) which he called *Mishneh Torah*, and the composition that he wrote in the language of Ishmael (Arabic), which he called *Guide of the Perplexed*—reached the great, honorable and mighty scholars, teachers of Torah, men of wisdom and understanding, the scholars of Lunel .... And during his life-time he received their delightful letters and their wonderful questions. From their words it was apparent to him, of blessed memory, that they understood his books and they rejoiced in them. He too rejoiced that his words had reached someone who understood them.... He wrote to them responsa to their questions, and he responded to their words to honor and glorify them, as was appropriate to them." (*Milhamot ha-Shem* [Wars of the Lord] [Jerusalem: Mossad Harav Kook Publishing, n.d.), 52–53.)
90 Shailat, *Iggrot ha-Rambam*, vol. I, 228–30.
91 Shailat, *Iggrot ha-Rambam*, vol. II, 436.
92 Davidson (*Maimonides*, 72) listed some of Maimonides' comments about illness, citing S. Goitein (*Mediterranean Society*, vol. 5, 243–45): "Whether the statement is to be taken literally must remain open, since accounts of lengthy physical disorders resulting from grief were something of a topos in his day."
93 See Shailat, *Iggrot ha-Rambam*, vol. II, 511–54, for the text of the letter and his discussion regarding the various segments of the letter, its composition, and dating.
94 Alexander Marx, "Texts by and about Maimonides," *Jewish Quarterly Review* XXV (1935): 371–428; see 376–77, as cited in Twersky, *Introduction to the Code*, 4–5, note 5.
95 Davidson, *Maimonides*, 432–33.
96 Blau, *Teshuvot ha-Rambam*, vol. III, 57, line 8, follows MSS Paris 18, which here has the word "very," which does not appear in the book of Esther.
97 Given that Maimonides wished to declare the essential value of the study of *hokhmah*, Twersky suggests that his reference to "sciences as handmaidens should be interpreted to refer to the ancillary sciences ... i.e., logic and related arts. *Hokhmah* per se, the core of metaphysics, is not alien." Twersky, *Introduction*, 499, note 367.
98 The longest chapter in Prof. Twersky's magnificent *Introduction to the Code of Maimonides* (chap. 6) is entitled "Law and Philosophy." He explores Maimonides "as jurisprudent and philosopher simultaneously ..." and that "his importance is to be assessed generally in terms of the scope and profundity of his achievement, and particularly in terms of the unprecedented extent to which he amalgamated these disciplines and commitments." (356–57)
99 This section dealing with Responsum 315 is adapted from my article, "Torah U'Madda and the Brain Death Debate," in *Halakhic Realities: Collected Essays on Brain Death* (Jerusalem: Koren Publishers, 2015), 349–91; see especially 382–86.
100 I. Twersky pointed out (*Introduction*, 56, note 89) that R. Saadia Gaon had previously ruled that a missing upper jaw is considered "treifah"; thus, Maimonides' opinion—although not identified with R. Saadia Gaon's prior ruling—was not a totally new decision.

101 Rabbeinu Yitzhak bar Sheshet (Rivash), *Sheilot U'Tshuvot* [Responsa of the Rivash], vol. II (Jerusalem: Machon Jerusalem, 5753/1992/3, 662–63, Responsum 447.
102 Rivash, *Sheilot U'Tshuvot*, vol. II, 512, Responsum 377.
103 In his Responsum 44 (ibid., vol. I, 49), he cited and strongly endorsed the opinion of R. Asher ben Yehiel (Responsum 31, section 9) who advised against legal decision making solely based upon a reading of the MT without full knowledge of the relevant Talmudic sources upon which Maimonides based his decision.
104 See Abraham M. Hershman, *Rabbi Isaac ben Sheshet Perfet and His Times* (New York: Jewish Theological Seminary, 1943), 78.
105 See also Responsum 251 of the Rivash (*Sheilot U'Tshuvot*, vol. I, 321), in which he stated that "The Torah contradicted these doctors."

Maimonides' position regarding the upper mandible is problematic. Commentators from all periods attempted to resolve this decision. Many noted that his inclusion of a missing upper mandible within his list of seventy types of "treifot" (Laws of Slaughter 8:23 and 10:9, subsection 52) seems to contradict his declared principle that "one is not allowed to add to these 'treifot' at all" since they were "calculated by the scholars of the early generations and the courts of Israel agreed upon them"; he also stated there that "even if it becomes known to us through the medium of healing [sciences] that the animal will not ultimately expire" we do not alter the traditional list but follow "what the scholars calculated (Laws of Slaughter, end chap. 10)."

Rashba (*Torat HaBayit*; as quoted in *Keseph Mishneh*, to MT, Laws of Slaughter 8:23) was impressed with Maimonides' decision regarding the upper jaw but he wished to ponder it further since this kind of "treifah" had not been included in the Mishna nor had it been presented in the Talmud. *Keseph Mishneh* wrote that Rashba's objection was resolved by Maimonides' explanation in his responsum to Lunel that this abnormality was included within the Mishnaic concept that any kind of defect that would not allow the animal to survive is deemed "treif." Thus, it is not a new kind of "treifah."

Davidson (*Maimonides*, 222, note 141), citing Jacob S. Levinger (*Darke ha-Mahshaba ha-Hilkatit shel ha-Rambam*; Jerusalem: Magnes Press 1965), states that "Maimonides can never be seen to set a norm in open opposition to the classic rabbinic sources." But Levinger himself (*Darke ha-Mahshaba*, 140) states that Maimonides conclusion was a commentary to the Talmudic sources based upon his knowledge of animal anatomy, and he also noted Maimonides' remarks that "treifot" are not to be derived from medical science.

Davidson (*Maimonides*, 222, note 141) here also cites I. H. Weiss, "Toledot ha-Rab Rabbenu Moshe ben Maimon," in *Bet Talmud I* (Jerusalem: Carmiel, 1881), who considered Maimonides' position regarding the upper jaw as an instance in which he had defined Jewish law based upon science.

In my opinion, the attempt to read Maimonides' law as a natural commentary to the Mishnah is unconvincing. The Lunel scholars, Rabad and Rivash, clearly held that to be a forced interpretation.
106 Blau, *Teshuvot ha-Rambam*, Responsum 287, vol. II, 539–40.
107 Ibid., vol. II, 593–95.
108 Ibid., Responsum 300, vol. II, 558–59.
109 Shailat, *Iggrot ha-Rambam*, vol. I (documents 18, 19, 20, 22, 25) contains communications between Maimonides and the Babylonia scholars. Also, see the entries under "Geonim" in Twersky, *Introduction to the Code*, 613, regarding Maimonides' attitude to the Geonim of the previous centuries. See also Davidson, *Maimonides*, 550, especially the citations there of various comments regarding the Geonic writings.

110 In addition to the three examples cited here, see also Blau, *Teshuvot ha-Rambam*, vol. II, 560, Responsum 302: "From your words its seems to me that there are some words missing in your [edition of the] book. This is the [correct] version of the book...."
111 Ibid., vol. II, 585-6.
112 Ibid., Responsum 354, vol. II, 630-31.
113 Ibid., vol. II, 713.
114 Unfortunately, we are not aware of any further contact with these men. No other communications are extant.
115 Similarly, at the conclusion of a set of responsa to R. Ephraim of Tyre and his pupils (Responsa 119-150), Maimonides wrote (in 1177): "This includes what R. Ephraim ... asked, and everything that you (i.e., his pupils) asked; we have already responded regarding these [matters]. May the Omnipresent have compassion upon him and may He bless you [plural; i.e., the pupils], and may He assist us all to engage in His commandments...." (Blau, *Teshuvot ha-Rambam*, vol. I, 286.)
116 For example, in a letter (written around 1191-92) to his beloved pupil, Joseph ben Judah, Maimonides offered a candid and revealing admission about his arrogant and pugnacious treatment of disputants during his youth. His pupil Joseph lived in Syria at that time, which was under the authority of the Baghdad Gaon, Samuel bar Eli (died 1194), who served as the head of the academy there for thirty years. Joseph was incensed at the abuse his Master suffered in public disputes with Samuel over some of Maimonides' writings. He wrote his Master that he wished to defend his name and his important works that had come under attack.

In a most revealing and personal letter, Maimonides urged his pupil to resist the temptation to enter the fray. He wrote that he understood what motivated Joseph to engage in this dispute because he too, in his youth, had a penchant for contentious exchanges. He reminisced before Joseph about cases in his early years in which "my disputants were made to cry by my tongue and my pen; by my tongue, if they were in my presence; by my pen, if they were distant." (Shailat, *Iggrot ha-Rambam*, vol. I, 419-22).

Maimonides had dedicated the *Guide* to Joseph and he once wrote him, "If I only had you that would be sufficient...." (Ibid., vol. I, 301, lines 13-14.) Given their relationship, it is understandable why he would have been so self-revealing and self-effacing in this letter to his pupil.
117 This letter is found in ibid., vol. II, 557-59. See also his introduction to the letter on 555-56.
118 See note 26, above.
119 Narbonne, Montpellier, Marseilles, etc. Maimonides alluded to the surrounding Provencal cities. Interestingly, he made no mention of the scholars and Torah centers in Northern France and Germany.
120 The irony of this correspondence is that the Provencal community became, in the coming century, the locus of the anti-Maimonidean controversy. Despite the admiring support of R. Jonathan and his circle during the waning of the twelfth century, later Provencal Jews did not share their admiration for Maimonides' many "strange wives."
121 See Hayyim Schirmann, "Ha-Rambam ve-ha-Shirah ha-'Ivrit'" [The Rambam and Hebrew Poetry; in Hebrew], *Moznaim* 3 (1935): 433-36.
122 Another possible contributing factor to Maimonides' position on poetry is Aristotle's attitude toward poetics. I did not examine the place of Aristotle's position on Maimonides since it was beyond the scope of this work.

123 Throughout this section, all citations from Maimonides' *Commentary on the Mishnah* are my translations of his work published by Mossad Harav Kook, Jerusalem, 5737 (1976–77).
124 Maimonides, *Commentary on the Mishnah*, vol. II, Sanhedrin, chap. 10, 140–41.
125 In the concluding chapter of his *Guide of the Perplexed*, Maimonides provided four interpretations of the term "*hokhmah*." (See Shlomo Pines, trans., *Guide of the Perplexed*, [Chicago: University of Chicago Press, 1963], vol. II, chap. 54, 632–36.) It is not clear how he used that term here. See also Davidson (*Maimonides*, 231, note 181), who lists various terms that are interpreted variously in his writings.
126 Also, the inclusion of Ben Sira on the banned list is problematic. See comments by Yosef Qafih, *Commentary on the Mishnah* (Jerusalem: Mossad Harav Kook, 1963–68) ad loc.
127 See Qafih (*Commentary on the Mishnah*, vol. II, Sanhedrin 10:1, note 12), 141, who notes that Maimonides makes no distinction between any type of poetry or subject matter. He cites the passage in *Iggeret* Unit 6: "it is well known that Maimonides was not a lover of "sharim v'sharot" (male/female singers; i.e., poets—the phrase in the letter to R. Jonathan), as he wrote in his responsum…." Qafih then refers the reader to a passage about poetry in the *Guide*, which will be analyzed shortly here.
128 Maimonides, *Commentary on the Mishnah*, vol. II, Avot, 272–74.
129 See note 119, above.
130 Blau, *Teshuvot ha-Rambam*, vol. II, Responsum 207, 363–66.
131 Ibid., Responsum 254, 465–68.
132 Ibid., 467–68.
133 Maimonides, *Guide*, I, chap. 2, 24.
134 Ibid., chap. 5, 29.
135 Twersky, *Introduction to the Code of Maimonides*, 482.
136 *Guide*, I, chap. 59, 140–41.
137 Ibid., 140.
138 Ibid., 141.
139 Twersky, *Introduction to the Code of Maimonides*, 250, note 29, regarding Radbaz, *T'shuvot*, vol. III (New York: 1947), 645, who wrote that Maimonides' target in this section of the *Guide* was Ibn Gabirol. See also the lengthy and comprehensive critique of "piyyut" and Eleazar ha-Kallir by Ibn Ezra (to Ecclesiastes 5:1).
140 In Nina Salaman's Introduction to her *Selected Poems of Jehudah Halevi* (Philadelphia: Jewish Publication Society, 1974 edition, xvi–xvii), she writes that "…Halevi has attained the highest honour to which a writer can aspire—the esteem of his peers. Harizi, the Hebrew poet-critic of a generation near his own, describes him as supremely inimitable, as one who "broke into the treasure-house of song," and who, going out again, "shut the gate behind him." His love-songs, his prayers, his epistles are all alike "drawn from the Holy Spirit."
141 See Benedict, "Torah-Centre in Provence," especially 92–93 and 99 regarding the respective methodologies of study in Spanish and Provencal centers.
142 Benjamin of Tudela (Marcus N. Adler, ed., *The Itinerary of Benjamin of Tudela* [London: Oxford University Press, 1907], 2) described Narbonne as a "city pre-eminent for learning; thence the Torah (Law) goes forth to all countries. Sages and great and illustrious men abide there." He said of Lunel: "…there is a congregation of Israelites who study the Law day and night (p. 3)." Also, see Benedict, "Torah-Centre in Provence," 85–109.

143 See S. D. Goitein, *Mediterranean Society*, vol. V, 448–68, and *Encyclopedia Judaica*, vol. 10, 356, under "Judah Halevi."
144 See Jeffrey L. Rubenstein, "Violence," in *The Culture of the Babylonian Talmud* (Baltimore: Johns Hopkins University Press, 2003), 54–66.
145 Halevi complimented the Narbonne *Iggeret* as "Who is she who shines through like the moon," which is an adaptation of the biblical verse which has "dawn" rather than "moon." He altered the text to fit the rhyme sequence.
146 The structure of this letter was consistent with the epistolary form as described above by Baneth, *Iggrot ha-Rambam*, 10, and which was identified in both Maimonides' letters. See the discussion of Baneth, pp. 35–36.
147 B. Z. Benedict, "Torah-Centre in Provence," 99. Also, see I. Ta-Shema, "Ibn Migash, Joseph ben Meir Ha-Levi," *Encyclopedia Judaica*, vol. 8, 1188–89.
148 See Salo W. Baron, *A Social and Religious History of the Jews*, vol. VI (New York: Columbia University Press, 1971), 84. This would be another valuable connection between Halevi and Maimonides. However, there is no evidence that Halevi was a student at Lucena. In addition, he does not display in his works extensive and advanced Talmud training, nor do his colleagues and those who tribute him refer to him as "Rav" or a title that would suggest significant rabbinic training. (From a written correspondence from Prof. Raymond Scheindlin.)

In addition to the letter to Narbonne, which Halevi composed on behalf of Ibn Migas, he also composed an elegy in memory of Ibn Migas when he died.
149 N. Wieder, "Judah Ibn Shabbetai's Burnt Book," *Metsudah*, vol. 2 (Dec. 1943), 128–29. The invasion of the Almohads drove Maimonides and his family from Cordova and the Lucena academy to Toledo, which is largely where Meir taught and where R. Jonathan studied. Under Meir's leadership there, it attracted students from all over Spain as well as Provence.
150 MT, *Laws of Borrowing and Pledges*, 5:6. See Malachi ha-Kohen, "Rules regarding Maimonides," part II, section 32, *Yad Malachi* (Przemysl, 1877), 186: "Whenever Rambam states in his Hibbur—'Thus my Masters ruled'—he refers to Rav Alfasi and Rav Yehosef Halevi, of blessed memory…." But see note 152. Also, see Shailat, *Iggrot ha-Rambam*, vol. I, 115, note to line 9, and Davidson, *Maimonides*, 78–79.
151 J. Kafih edition (Jerusalem: Mosad Harav Kook, 1963), vol. I, 25.
152 Responsum 251, Blau, *Teshuvot ha-Rambam*, vol. II, 459.
153 Translation by Twersky in his *Introduction to the Code*, 7. See Davidson, *Maimonides*, 78–79, note 19, for numerous comments by Maimonides regarding Ibn Migas.
154 *Yad Malachi* (ha-Kohen, "Rules regarding Maimonides," part II, section 32) properly interprets Maimonides' praise of Rav Alfasi and Rav Yehosef Halevi to reflect his high regard for their teaching and their influence on his MT. He provides the correct chronology to demonstrate that Maimonides could not have studied under Migas. He states that this error is derived from a responsum by Tashbetz (*Sefer ha-Tashbetz* [Jerusalem: Machon Yerushalayim, 5758/1997–98], vol. I, Responsum 72, 158–59).

www.ingramcontent.com/pod-product-compliance
Lightning Source LLC
Chambersburg PA
CBHW061944220426
43662CB00012B/2021